the ODYSSEY *of* MRS. NAOMI BILLINGSLEY

the
ODYSSEY
of
MRS. NAOMI BILLINGSLEY

SALLY STEVENS

atmosphere press

CONTENTS

Chapter 1:   The New Patient.. 3

Chapter 2:   The Energizing Elevator.......................... 8

Chapter 3:   The "To South America" Exit 11

Chapter 4:   Garbage Review Therapy 15

Chapter 5:   Volunteering Can Be Hazardous
             (To Patients) 22

Chapter 6:   The Sad Cake Event at
             The Music Festival 25

Chapter 7:   Brother Goodfellow and the Flood 31

Chapter 8:   The Fish Scale & the Knight
             in Shining Armor 41

Chapter 9:   Lunch at The Cat & Fiddle Pub 47

Chapter 10: A More Romantic Life
             Through Landscaping......................... 54

Chapter 11: The Doctor Takes A Tumble............... 60

Chapter 12: The Flying Cows 66

Chapter 13: Early Tinnitus & The Peach Pit...................... 74

Chapter 14: The New Neighbors 78

Chapter 15: Leila Mae & The Brownies 82

Chapter 16: The Toucan & The Faceless Man.....................91

Chapter 17: Let's Write a Musical About Death.................. 95

Chapter 18: Leila Mae Leaves 98

Chapter 19: Billy Randall & the Reunion...................... 103

Chapter 20: Physician, Heal Thyself................................112

Chapter 1

the New Patient

Dr. Birnteller was somewhat befuddled by his new patient. Not that he would ever publicly disclose this, for he had his professional reputation to uphold, at least in his own mind. The degrees and certificates of honorable recognition that hung on his wall were tangible evidence of his respected position within the psychiatric community. The fact that among his past patients could be found a handful of eventually institutionalized souls, and a rumor (nothing more) of one tragic but (if true) obviously unavoidable suicide, was something that the good doctor worked hard at keeping under the radar. He was, if nothing else, conscientious.

He was always open, however, to new discoveries; alert to coming across in his practice some patient that might become the subject of a new study, a presentation to his comrades in the world of shared psychiatric revelations. Mrs. Naomi Billingsley certainly appeared to have the potential for being such a patient. The problem was that her symptoms fell somewhere within the grey area between psychiatric explanation and the supernatural or mystical, even bordering on a religious hysteria kind of evidence. This of course could be quite threatening to his professional respectability within the field of medical science. It might cause him to have to change fields altogether. Which, based on the success rate with his string of most recent patients, it occurred to him, might not be a bad idea.

He reviewed the notes from Mrs. Billingsley's last visit as he sat in the Eames chair, his feet resting on the desk in front of him: "Mrs. B. reports more frequent insights of late, and seems to have gotten past the discomfort of revealing her innermost thoughts. I have observed unusual symptoms, which, while viewed with normal clinical skepticism, are nonetheless fascinating to note. Patient arrived for appointment Friday with manifestations of open wounds on the backs of both hands. We discussed this phenomenon with objectivity for the better part of fifty minutes. It was apparent she suffered no discomfort from the wounds and would probably not even have noticed them, had I not pointed them out. First assumed they were charismatic in nature but corrected my diagnosis later, when droplets of blood were detected on the Naugahyde chaise. Note: Adjust patient's billing to cover cleaning of chaise."

The doctor's thoughts were interrupted by the flashing red light signaling the arrival of his patient. He arose to open the door to the inner office, and as he greeted Mrs. Billingsley, was alarmed at the sight of what appeared to be a fresh bullet wound in the woman's forehead. Yes, a clean shot, it appeared. No longer bleeding, thank goodness, since he had had the carpet cleaned only a month ago. Then he reflected upon past observations of this patient, and allowed for the possibility that this might have been a self-inflicted emotional wound resulting from a deep depression so profoundly felt that the patient manifested it physically. Yes, they could explore this possibility. Mrs. Billingsley seemed not at all disturbed by the bullet hole. Things obviously were beginning to move into high gear.

The doctor waited diplomatically for the right opening and then chose his words carefully. "Mrs. Billingsley," he asked in a clinical, matter-of-fact tone, "have you become aware yet this morning of the fresh bullet wound in your forehead?"

"Oh, that..." said Mrs. Billingsley. "It was probably my husband taking potshots at me again, Doctor. I am handling it so much better than I used to, thanks to your excellent help. Usually I come right back with a few of my own, which is probably why he was lying prone on the driveway as I left this morning."

Rather than upset her with more insensitive inquiries, the doctor took a moment to consider quietly the various possible explanations for this phenomenon. Perhaps, he thought, the wound might be the beginning of a "third eye," a further expansion of her rapidly growing mystical consciousness. He didn't know a great deal about the third eye theory, but it seemed logical.

This speculative pursuit was interrupted by a knock on the door of his office.

"Please excuse me." The doctor got up from the swivel chair, went to the door, and was startled to find two uniformed police officers standing there. They presented him with a search warrant.

"Good morning, sir. Please excuse the interruption, but we are in pursuit of a fugitive, a suspect in a domestic violence case which is reported to have ended in a fatality, and we must ask you to step aside while we conduct a search of the premises."

The policemen stepped into the inner office and approached the woman stretched out on the chaise. "Are you Mrs. Naomi Billingsley of 322 River Road?" asked one of the officers authoritatively.

"Why, yes I am, officer...is there a problem?"

"I'm sorry, ma'am, but you'll have to come to the station with us. We're taking you into custody as a suspect in the death of your husband, who was discovered lying in your driveway earlier this morning by a neighbor."

The doctor started to step forward, instinctively protective of his patient, but was stopped by the second officer's drawn revolver.

"We must ask you not to interfere, sir."

Interference, of course, was the last thing on the doctor's mind. His therapeutic task, as he repeatedly told himself, was not to alter the course of events, but to provide deeper understanding of why they occurred, and to encourage acceptance of all things on a psychic as well as physical level.

"Mrs. Billingsley, do not be alarmed," he gently cautioned as he stepped away from the chaise. "Forces seem to have gathered to keep us from our work today, but such an interruption into one's journey of the psyche can only be temporary. You have my number at home. Please feel free to call me upon your release from custody."

Mrs. Billingsley got up, straightened her clothing, picked up her handbag, and smiled at the officers.

"Thank you, Doctor. You are too kind, as always. These young men are just doing their jobs. I feel a certain peacefulness about all this, since I am quite sure Mr. Billingsley was still breathing as I drove past him in the driveway. These little moments happen, you know, in the course of a marriage, and can usually be cleared up with a bit of heart-to-heart communication."

Mrs. Billingsley was taken to the police station, booked on suspicion of manslaughter, and placed in a small cell apart from the other inmates, as she had no past criminal record and really offered no physical resistance to her arrest. Eventually, of course, she was released from jail after the misunderstanding was cleared up.

Well, "released" is not entirely accurate either. As she described it to Dr. Birnteller on her next visit, a mysterious explosion had shaken the city jail later that afternoon, causing such damage that inmates had to be transported to the county facility. During the ensuing confusion with the transport, Mrs. Billingsley slipped quietly away and took the Number 17 bus home. She was better prepared to take advantage of the confusion than the other inmates because, of course, she had been expecting the explosion. She'd been sitting quietly on her cot, trying to imagine what kind of disturbance could possibly disrupt the security of a jail situation, when suddenly the walls began to shake.

Upon returning home, she and Mr. Billingsley cleared up their differences, standing arm in arm together in the driveway, looking down at the chalk outline of his previously immobilized form. Funny, they said, how one could laugh at these things that seem so deadly serious in the heat of battle.

To make up for her part in the spat, Mrs. Billingsley prepared deep-fried cod and flounder, Mr. Billingsley's favorite. All in all, they experienced a highly convivial evening.

Chapter 2

the Energizing Elevator

The following day, Mrs. Billingsley prepared to dress for her morning appointment with the doctor. The bullet wound in her forehead was not entirely healed yet, so in order to escape the rude stares with which she had been plagued the day before, she carefully selected her ensemble. She dressed in a purple and beige tweed suit with velvet collar, usually reserved for luncheons with the Ladies Auxiliary. It was the only outfit she owned that looked smart when set off with the small black hat and nose-tipping veil. Perched on the side of the hat was a small, black-feathered bird carcass with shining glass eyes that stared at an odd angle over her shoulder. Normally she felt just a tad uncomfortable about the bird, but today it seemed a useful distraction.

Mr. Billingsley was standing in the driveway as she left, washing the last of the bloodstains away from the chalk outline with the garden hose. She noted sadly that the chalk outline was disappearing as well. Something about the presence of the chalk outline had definitely lifted the neighborhood above its usual tedium.

The traffic was light driving into town, but in the elevator of the medical building Mrs. Billingsley was gripped with a new and rather interesting terror. She became momentarily fixated on the possibility of the elevator getting stuck between floors, wedged indefinitely in some never-land between eight and nine, or seventeen and eighteen. She began to speculate about how long a fifty-seven-year-old woman with nothing to read or eat could remain alive and sane alone in an elevator. She wondered if anyone would notice that the elevator was missing, or if they would just attribute the gathering crowds below to the usual slow service. She wondered whether elevator musical selections began to repeat themselves after six or seven hours, and she wondered if she was still agile enough to climb unassisted through the elevator roof. There would always be something to deal with, she thought, even if it wasn't real. She found this thought somewhat comforting, in a way she was sure other people would find hard to understand.

Then the elevator jolted to a stop, and the doors opened. She had the brief sensation that the ocean was rushing in from the hallway, bringing with it fishes and seaweed, seashells, and bits of broken Coke bottles worn smooth by waves. Yes, always something to deal with, she thought to herself as she carefully stepped over the broken bottles and made a mental note to take the grandchildren to the shore on the first sunny day of summer break. Then she remembered she had no grandchildren. But perhaps she could take someone else's grandchildren.

She was late for her appointment by two minutes, and rushed down the hall toward the doctor's office, the familiar doorways and nameplates a blur in her peripheral vision. Outside the door, she began to experience a subtle, convoluted sensation, as if her body had been turned inside out. It was at that moment she realized she was standing inside the office on the other side of the closed door, without ever having opened it.

The doctor looked up. It was no more than he had been expecting. Wisely, he had not filled her hour even though to the best of his conscious knowledge she was still behind bars. He managed to overlook her failure to knock preceding her entry.

"Good morning, Mrs. Billingsley. There's a bit of kelp dragging from the heel of your shoe. Would you mind removing it before you lie down?"

"Of course, Doctor, how careless of me," she said as she scraped away the seaweed. "I can't tell you how energized I am by my visits with you. And you have the most fascinating building. Absolutely brimming over with life forces."

"Now...where were we?" He tried to hide his disappointment. He had never seen an enlightened being sporting a dead bird on her head. The brilliant future he had been reading between the scribbled lines of her unconscious mind had faded just a bit. And the foolish little veil obscured the forehead wound he had so eagerly wished to re-evaluate. Despite the broadly accepted fact that fashion is a superficial aspect of life, on this day it also seemed very revealing of possible character shortcomings.

Mrs. Billingsley sensed his dismay, and gently reminded him that events themselves were not problematic, but only one's view of them, as he had so wisely shared during one of their earlier sessions. The rest of the hour was relatively uneventful, though they touched on an interesting and revealing discussion of the symbolic meaning of the sea and the pull of the tides as it related to birth and rebirth, psychically speaking. Mrs. Billingsley casually mentioned in a comforting tone as she departed the office that tomorrow she would probably not be wearing a dead bird.

Chapter 3

the "To South America" Exit

The freeway was congested as Mrs. Billingsley drove home from the doctor's office. Her mind drifted as it had a tendency to do whenever she was behind the wheel, and then it came suddenly and sharply back into focus as she caught sight of an exit sign that read "To Central America."

Why not? she thought. With the heavy traffic, she could be stuck on the freeway for hours, and Mr. Billingsley did have his tango lesson on Tuesday evenings. She was certain to be back by the time he returned. Then she remembered she had taken the same exit several weeks ago and had gotten hopelessly lost in the jungles of El Salvador. The ramp curved across Mexico to the southeast and emptied out near the southern border of Guatemala.

She recalled having found the rush of imminent danger quite stimulating, and made a note of how rarely she allowed herself the experience. However, considering how the anti-American sentiment had become more apparent and how the bullets had passed closer and closer to her car, she decided that this time she would drive on toward South America. She found the "Venezuela" exit, turned off the freeway, and headed for town, where she passed the small restaurant that she remembered had served a most impressive steak. The tiny mice scampering about the floor had been an interesting curiosity, but linger she mustn't, or she would not have time for the rest of the trip. She made a quick stop, enjoyed "el bistec, vuelta y vuelta" prepared to perfection.

"Muchas gracias, senor," she said, and tipped him generously. She also left a bit of biscuit on the floor for the mice.

Then she scurried on, heading farther south. As she drove through the streets of Buenos Aires, she was fascinated by the public pronouncements of affection for Eva Peron that still remained, scribbled on walls and deserted buildings, preserved from so many years ago. She marveled at the mysterious power of sexuality, even in politics, and considered the irony of the Madonna-Whore fixation that had hypnotized the entire, very Catholic population of Argentina. Probably it was a useful thing, she thought. It kept the people's minds off of their own terrible poverty, and also off of the unbearable humidity.

She noted with appropriate respect the guards on the street corners with their automatic weapons, and wondered for a moment how that would work back in Mayfield. Given the present mindset of the city council, she wouldn't be at all surprised if, upon her return, she would find a few armed officers strategically placed. After all, the conservative vote did seem to be on the rise of late. But there would be time to ponder the politics of her own nation. Right now, she was here to soak up the journey.

She decided to circle back northward and soon found herself winding up the steep mountain road toward the statue of Christ The Redeemer of the Andes. The huge statue stood, its arms outreached, welcoming all the souls within sight of it. As she reached the top of the mountain, enormous, magnificently-colored butterflies gathered and danced outside the car window. In the open area at the base of the statue itself, the atmosphere became strangely Dali-esque. Native people of the area were scattered about, hawking necklaces they had made by stringing dozens of huge cows' teeth together on brightly-colored string. From a distance the necklaces bore an artistic air and could almost pass for ivory. After all, they were certainly no more bizarre than wearing ivory, if one truly thought about it. She purchased several. Then she began to wonder if they were cow teeth or horse teeth. This bothered her a bit more. She hoped they were cow teeth shipped over from Venezuela after the cows had produced those delicious steaks like the one she enjoyed earlier. She hated to imagine anything being killed for its teeth alone. She thought about asking the vendors the source of the necklaces, but decided that ambiguity was a better option for peace of mind.

The natives were also selling carved crucifixes. The wood was beautiful and highly polished, and though Mrs. Billingsley was not one to make public display of her religious convictions she bought several, thinking they would make nice Easter gifts. She could place them in cheerful plastic baskets lined with pink cellophane grass and jellybeans, or chocolate eggs and bunnies. It would take the sting out of the whole issue of the Crucifixion and somewhat mollify the sadomasochistic tone of the holiday.

After wandering through the crowds for a while, she gathered her crucifixes and teeth necklaces and drove down the mountain, back out through the jungles and eastward, on to the romantic city of Rio de Janeiro. She stopped at the beautiful Copacabana Palace Hotel overlooking the beach. It was dusk, the perfect time for a cocktail break, and after freshening her makeup and fluffing her hair, she left her car with the parking valet and walked into the lounge.

There, seated at the bar, was the handsome vaquero whose advances she had resisted on her last trip. But Mr. Billingsley *did* have his tango lessons, which was his chosen form of romantic self-expression, and life is short, she thought. The handsome vaquero stood and gazed longingly at her through dark, passionate eyes, his recognition of her enlivening his expression. It was too much to resist. They left together, and the handsome vaquero showed her the nightlife. They took a swim off the beaches of Copacabana and then enjoyed a very brief but inevitable affair. She was a little uncomfortable at first, experiencing such intimacy with a perfect stranger, and made an attempt at resisting his advances. But after all, he *was* such a *perfect* stranger, and the moonlight, the Latin rhythms, and the time change all combined to distance her from reality enough to allow her to take the plunge. And these temporary, spontaneous fixations are what help us get through the tedium of life, she thought. It would be awkward talking with the doctor about this, but she felt he would have the clinical skills necessary to understand.

Suddenly Mrs. Billingsley realized the hours had flown, and it was time to head home. It was not easy saying goodbye. Always, with these journeys, Mrs. Billingsley was tempted to linger. But she had responsibilities at home, so flee she must, with one lingering, tearful embrace.

She managed to get back on the freeway just as a soft mist began to hit the windshield. Soon heavier drops fell, and then wind in great gusts. Before long the expanse before her was covered in snow, heavy blankets of it piling up along the sides of the road. She marveled at the rapid passing of the seasons and turned on the car heater and window defroster. The faintest hint of Drakkar Noir cologne floated through her sensory memory, but the dark eyes of the handsome vaquero were fading. The passions of Rio drifted far behind, and likewise, the climate. Interesting, she thought, how we adapt to our surroundings. Dr. Birnteller would be proud. She hoped Mr. Billingsley would be waiting with tales of his tango class and a hot cup of Nestlé cocoa.

Chapter 4

Garbage Review Therapy

It had been awkward carrying the huge plastic garbage bag through the lobby of the building and on into the elevator, but the idea had been inspirational, and she was anxious to get started with the doctor. Mrs. Billingsley sat in the waiting room of Dr. Birnteller's office, the large bundle she'd brought with her resting on the floor next to her chair. She was in her sixth week of therapy, still getting used to the process but priding herself on having plunged in so bravely, and the subconscious insights were beginning to pour in.

It was already ten minutes past the hour when the doctor finally opened the waiting room door and motioned her inside. Then, in a distracted manner, he returned to his chair, barely lifting his eyes from the papers in his lap. They both sat in silence for a few moments, and, a bit puzzled, she finally decided to address the situation.

"Good morning, Doctor. I hope I'm not disturbing you?"

"Not at all, Mrs. Billingsley. The goal of our time together is to provide you with a sense of total well-being and acceptance. Nothing you do could disturb me. I'm getting quite used to you. This is your hour. Disturb away!"

"Well, I was hoping to discuss an event which occurred

last night, and which was most peculiar, though not entirely unfamiliar."

"Very well. You must trust that this journey of the self will be accomplished, all in good time. It's what we are here for. Excuse me for just a moment..." He started to dig for something in the file drawer, projecting an attitude of not wishing to be disturbed despite his protestations to the contrary. Mrs. Billingsley was puzzled by his uncharacteristic disinterest. Perhaps he was trying a different psychological method, she thought.

Finally he lifted his gaze. "And speaking of a good time, Mrs. Billingsley, did you have one?" he asked.

"One what, Doctor?"

"Last night..." replied the doctor. "A good time? Last night? *Ever?*" He lowered his glasses and glowered at her over the frames.

Mrs. Billingsley felt herself growing smaller and smaller. She imagined herself getting lost in the creases of the chaise. She imagined the doctor having to search for her as if she were fallen change from the pockets of some previous, more significant and highly valued patient. Smaller and smaller, she envisioned herself lost on a safari, peering over the top of the thick carpet pile as if it were the wild grasses of Borneo and she was laboriously making her way through it toward the door.

"Well?" he said, continuing to glower.

She flashed for a moment on her adventures in South America with the handsome vaquero, but since she had not yet shared that with the doctor, she backed away from the embarrassment and shame that it threatened briefly to trigger. He did seem wise and all-knowing, but he really could hardly breach the doctor-patient confidentiality with materials she'd not yet shared.

She managed to gather her composure and replied to his question. "Yes, Doctor. Yes, I did have a good time. The details don't really matter, and though I have conflicted feelings about some of my activities, I believe it was all for the best. I'm not used to having a good time, Doctor."

"Would you expand upon your answer, please?" he asked, but then turned his attention back to the file drawer.

Mrs. Billingsley clung to the belief that the good doctor had her best interests at heart. There was a lesson here, if she could just grasp it.

"Well?" he said as he picked up the Rubik's Cube he kept on the desk to amuse himself with during long periods of such silences with some of his patients.

"Where was I, please?" Her voice was weak and distant, and she kept looking at her watch, but it had gotten smaller too, and was impossible to read without her glasses. She was beginning to feel like a target. She was not quite sure how to proceed. The doctor seemed to be trying a new therapeutic approach. It felt to her as though the conversation had deteriorated into a dance, wherein she, the patient, desperately tried to capture his attention and he, the physician, weaved and dodged, escaping her every vain attempt. He definitely seemed to be pursuing something unrelated to her psychiatric well-being. It was time to bring things back into focus. She summoned her best energy.

"As you, more profoundly than anyone, know, Doctor, there are two sides to every question. There is the inside and the outside, metaphysically speaking of course. Would you excuse me for a moment, please?"

She stepped out into the waiting room and retrieved the huge plastic garbage bag she had brought with her, dragging it back into the office.

"This bag is full of garbage, Doctor, and I think our garbage reveals a great deal about our lives. It occurred to me that perhaps with your help, we could go even deeper, and that the garbage might be used to reveal something also about the subconscious level of one's life."

Uncertain as to how the doctor would respond to the rather

untidy prospect, she nonetheless began to slowly remove the garbage from the bag, item by item.

Apparently with this move, she had at least wrested the lead away from him in the dance of distraction. The doctor closed his file drawer and set aside the Rubik's Cube. Though inwardly horrified at the mess unfolding on his carpet, he was maintaining a calm exterior. He even reached over to hold the bag open for her. He had to acknowledge that it certainly did reflect creative thinking on her part. And who knows, she just may have stumbled upon something useful.

Mrs. Billingsley tentatively began her dissertation.

"These are pork chop bones, Doctor. We had them two nights ago. I have had to abandon my commitment to veganism and the pursuit of spiritual enlightenment through dietary means, due to the fact that Mr. Billingsley threatened me with divorce if he were faced with one more meal of mung bean sprouts and millet. I was devastated, of course, but perhaps there is something to be gained in cheerfully abandoning one's personal goals for the greater good of the tribe. He at any rate has been much more cheerful of late. And his tango technique has improved."

"Excellent, Mrs. Billingsley. That is, in regard to the tango. Please proceed."

"These torn bits of paper, Doctor, are the shredded pieces of my interrupted dreams. I have had the most extraordinary dreams, and awakened always in the early dawn to write them down in the most careful detail. Perhaps if I had slept longer, they might have come to fruition, but still I cannot part with them, for what is life if one abandons one's dreams? So, fearful that they be held up to ridicule, I have in a controlled way destroyed them, while still keeping them close. They are here, but not here, so to speak."

"What did we say about dreams the other day? They are often just the result of indigestion. But carry on..."

Mrs. Billingsley paused and wiped a tear from the corner

of her eye with a slightly used scrap of paper towel. The doctor noted her sorrow, but felt the time was not right to comment on it.

"These, Doctor," she exclaimed, bravely presenting a bulging shoebox tied with string, "are ticket stubs from all the films I have seen since 1970. They serve as a reminder of the lessons learned with other misguided souls who also learned all *they* know of life from the silver screen. I miss the warmth of that common bond, those somewhat aberrant lessons taken with strangers in the hallowed darkness. Look," as she pulled off the string and dug into the pile of old ticket stubs, "here is the ticket from *Jaws*...such a lesson about unexpected consequences, Doctor. I was never afraid of sharks until I saw that film, and as a result, I've managed to avoid being accosted by a shark for all these intervening years. I was so young then. Had I not overcome my fear, I might have carelessly allowed a shark to eviscerate me."

The doctor glanced longingly out of the corner of his eye at his Rubik's Cube, still sitting on his desk. Then he cleared his throat and turned his attention back to his patient.

"And here, *Star Wars*—another lesson in courage. Princess Leia. She dressed oddly, Doctor, just like I did as a girl, but still she managed to be accepted, in an interplanetary sort of way. I never mastered it in my daily life, but knew that should the need for interplanetary travel come up, I would be ready. I never worked up enough courage to try the hairdo. But—one step at a time, I'm sure you would agree. And oh, look—*Ferris Bueller's Day Off*. I never did quite get the point of that one. Obviously, Ferris was making a movie, so it was hardly his day off. Well, never mind. Sometimes you just have to write off your movie choices to youthful enthusiasm and peer pressure."

"*Ferris Bueller*, Mrs. Billingsley? You're referencing *Ferris Bueller's Day Off* as an example of clinical data, here in my office?" But he cleared his throat awkwardly, realized he had crossed the therapeutic line a bit out of his annoyance over the buildup of garbage on his office floor. "Excuse me, Mrs. Billingsley," he said in a conciliatory tone. "Please go on."

She maintained her focus and continued. "But now, today, isolated, alone in our living rooms, we've lost touch with the lessons to be learned from being part of a community. We practice only the art of isolation. The astonishing growth of online streaming and other gadgets has altered the course of mankind. Our only companions are the smiling faces on the screen who come into our homes to sell us toothpaste or Viagra, and we even shut them out with the remote control. It's so sad, Doctor. Sitting alone in our living rooms, how can we possibly know how to extract the life lessons?" She shook her head.

"Remember," the doctor said, trying to regain his professional composure, "ours is not to judge. Mankind will continue to make these technological advances with or without our support. Please just continue. What are those little brown things?"

"Oh. Yes, well, these are cherry pits, apricot pits, peach pits, and nectarine pits, Doctor. I spent the better part of last Wednesday canning preserves. I had intended to plant the pits along the driveway and surprise Mr. Billingsley next spring with lovely blossoms. But he, to surprise me, had the entire front yard surfaced in lovely grass-colored cement, so there was no place left to plant the pits. The concrete wouldn't have been my choice, but then we each have our own ways of expressing affection."

"How do you feel about that? The concrete, I mean..."

"Well, I hadn't really thought about it, Doctor. I suppose he..."

"I'm sorry, Mrs. Billingsley. I realize we've only scratched the surface of the abundant supply of garbage you've brought in, but I've just looked at my watch and admittedly, with a bit of relief—because honesty must come first in our relationship—I must point out that our hour is spent. Why don't we

THE ODYSSEY OF MRS. NAOMI BILLINGSLEY

utilize these remaining few moments to tidy up my office and bundle the garbage back into its plastic bag? Certain insights will occur in the doing of this mindless task, which would, I'm sure, be useful in our next session."

As Mrs. Billingsley was leaving his office, the doctor decided to step out on a therapeutic limb. "Just a minute, Mrs. Billingsley. Mind you, just a suggestion. You might consider bringing me pork chop bones with meat attached next time. Or some of the actual homemade preserves themselves. Just a suggestion. There is garbage, and then there is *garbage*. Our garbage is more valuable if it benefits those around us. I would look upon an upgrade as a possible indication that you were ready to move forward into the present, into *life*. Or at least to look eye to eye with the moment at hand. Rummaging through random rubble from the past does nothing but leave residual coffee grounds on my carpet. It's the origins of the rubble that count."

Mrs. Billingsley was too mortified to even say goodbye. What was it about her that people continually misinterpreted? She dragged the bag of garbage out the door, down the hall, and onto the elevator, where she abandoned it. It occurred to her that someone else might be able to retrieve it and use it for their own hour with the doctor. She wondered if he would recognize it as stolen garbage. She considered the little-known but highly insightful analytical theory that nothing means anything, really, on its own, and therefore the garbage was just a tool to unlock her subconscious. It could just as easily, then, be used to unlock someone else's subconscious. She could afford to be generous. But she felt somewhat depressed. We are such fragile creatures, she thought. If the doctor was going to be so unappreciative as to scold her for her best efforts, it was the last time she would go to the trouble of bringing him garbage.

Chapter 5

Volunteering Can Be Hazardous (*to* Patients)

Mrs. Billingsley felt a little bit better once she'd washed the coffee grounds off her hands in the women's restroom of Dr. Birnteller's building. The sun was pouring now through the glass door of the lobby area and its warmth took away the disappointment of the last hour and renewed her spirits, making her feel the day was still young and beckoning. She was learning that there would be good days and bad days, and she was willing to accept that. She stepped out onto the sidewalk, contemplating the options for passing the remainder of her afternoon.

Since the unfortunate embarrassment of having served Twinkies to the women of the Ladies Auxiliary as a joke, and their not realizing it was a joke, she couldn't face them, and so could eliminate their luncheon meeting as a possibility for the afternoon. And the Rotary Wives were really just the Ladies Auxiliary on a different afternoon, the same faces in a different restaurant. What to do? Of course. She would go by the hospital and drop in on her patients with the little cart of magazines, fresh fruit, and sundries. It would lift her spirits to be of service to other human beings.

Mrs. Billingsley drove across town to Mayfield Community Hospital and Urgent Care Center and parked in the Volunteers

Lot. She stopped just inside the hospital entrance at the Volunteer Guild Office to pick up her pink-and-white-striped pinafore and stock one of the carts with reading materials of relatively recent date. She added an assortment of gum, mints, personal hygiene items, and a delightful large basket of fresh fruit. Some of it was not so fresh, actually, so she put the bruised apples and one brown banana on the bottom of the pile. People seldom took the fruit anyway. It was more of a symbolic gesture than a sincere offering.

The activities at the hospital always managed to lift her spirits and make her feel useful, even authoritative, with an "in charge" kind of attitude. Sometimes just being vertical in the presence of so many horizontal people gave her confidence.

She set off at a good clip down the hall of the West Wing. She had noticed that the patients were rarely the same, from visit to visit. Fewer and fewer familiar faces smiled up at her from the tilted heads of their hospital beds. Modern medicine was either getting a lot better or a lot worse. In either case, it seemed to be working to her advantage because hardly any patients managed to make it through the entire collection of magazines during their stays.

As she passed Room 223 on the second floor, an urgent voice called out to her. "Mrs. Billingsley, may we see you for a moment?" She backed the cart up and stuck her head inside the door.

Two doctors in white hospital coats were comparing notes on two clipboards and arguing animatedly with one another across the bed of a patient, as if the patient himself were not present. The younger doctor spoke first.

"Mrs. Billingsley, we're having a devil of a time making sense of these charts. Perhaps you can settle an argument for us."

The patient was gazing up at them, a bewildered-looking man perhaps in his late sixties, with just the slightest hint of terror reflected in his eyes. Mrs. Billingsley smiled at him and patted his foot lovingly through the hospital blanket.

"There, there," she said gently, and then to the doctors, "What seems to be the problem?"

"Well, Dr. Simpkins contends that the patient's elevated temperature and stomach pains are indicative of the common flu, and I feel he has not taken into consideration the fact that his lunch order included a chili omelet, coconut caramel custard, and nine ounces of grapefruit juice, unsweetened...and that the thermostat for this room is set at eighty-seven degrees. Those facts would lead *me* to conclude that he is in fact suffering from gallstones. Removal would definitely get rid of the stomach pain, eventually. Now, surgery is also offering a special this week on gallstone removals, and we can throw in a rhinoplasty while he's under."

Mrs. Billingsley looked sternly at the two doctors and shook her head. Sometimes, alas, a persuasive argument could be made in support of Christian Science.

"Gentlemen, it takes little medical skill to see that both of *you* are suffering primarily from poor judgment. I would prescribe for this patient a strict diet of nothing but fresh kale, lightly steamed, and a seven-grain cereal. They may be mixed together or enjoyed separately, with a light topping of flax seed. Also be sure he has ten four-ounce glasses of diluted carrot juice daily, and no salt, except for that with which he is to brush his teeth every two hours. The patient should attempt to do twenty-five sit-ups on the hour, which should relieve the stomach pain."

The patient's face as Mrs. Billingsley spoke grew frozen in horror. "No, no," he cried weakly, and the blips on his monitoring device became erratic, darting wildly up and down in jagged lines. Then, slowly, they leveled out into one lone, continuous line with gentle beeps at even intervals. His eyes stared up at the ceiling and his sunken chest was still.

My. Some people just cannot handle the truth, thought Mrs. Billingsley, shaking her head disapprovingly as she pushed her cart resignedly toward the East Wing.

Chapter 6

the Sad Cake Event *at* *the* Music Festival

The teakettle's whistle interrupted Mrs. Billingsley's concentration as she sat at the breakfast table absorbing the news of the day. After preparing her customary cup of hot water with lemon juice and taking her ginkgo biloba, she returned her attention to the morning edition of the *Mayfield Daily Journal.* She had always been a very emotional reader, and generally, the news reaffirmed her most dearly held beliefs. Mrs. Billingsley embraced the concept of the oneness of mankind and clung to the belief that intrinsic goodness flowed from person to person. She devoutly wished to believe this. She had wept over the obituaries of perfect strangers as she read at her kitchen table the glowing accounts of their now sadly ended lives, and with equal sincerity she beamed at photographs of blushing brides. She felt a surge of personal pride when she read the latest accomplishments of each scientist, musician, artist, or, on rare occasion, honest politician whose achievements earned them a place on the front pages of the newspaper. In this way she experienced the embrace of all humanity and registered herself a part of the mainstream of life.

On this particular morning, however, she sat grim-faced as she read the horrifying account of the Mayfield Spring

Music Festival. Traditionally a happy, celebratory event held annually in the outdoor band shell in Oak Park, it was much looked forward to by the community as an opportunity to experience and support the latest up-and-coming young local conductors and composers who would make guest appearances with the local musicians. The festival was an all-day celebration of the arts and included morning and early evening concerts, with a relaxed afternoon in between for viewing the Arts and Crafts displays set up in booths on the rolling lawns and sampling the homemade pastries and soups provided by the Unitarian Church at the refreshment booths.

But on this particular morning, the sad words Mrs. Billingsley read on the front page of the newspaper shocked and horrified her. According to the article, sometime during the evening performance of the Mahler, there had begun a sudden exodus of some members of the audience, a handful here, a row of people there. At first folks assumed it might be an editorial comment on the choice of material or the performance quality, and the remaining audience stirred in a self-conscious and irritated manner. As the story unfolded, however, it was revealed that emergency care had been required, and after numerous stomach-pumpings and inquiries by the local police, it was discovered that the unsuspecting victims had succumbed to a batch of tainted carrot cake. Fortunately, the cake, a somewhat out-of-fashion dessert, had not been a hugely popular item. Upon further investigation, it was also learned that one of the volunteers, a deranged Unitarian, bitter, grief-stricken, and driven over the edge by his fifth successive rejection to his bid for Composer-in-Residence, had laced the carrot cake with liquid plant food. One of the women had seen him lurking at the back of the refreshment booth and remembered that he had picketed the grounds the previous year, which made him a prime suspect. That, along with his part-time position at the Mayfield Nursery and Garden Supply, which made the liquid plant food easily accessible.

The disappointment Mrs. Billingsley experienced reading this morbid tale was devastating. This action reflected badly on the entire family of man. She scanned the newspaper for some bit of positive news, something that would offset the ugliness and renew her faith and positive outlook. She found nothing. She reflected for a moment and had to admit that lately there had really been little in the news to keep her positive view of the world in focus. Only a few days earlier, there had been a report of a riot following Mayfield High School's victory over Fall River on the basketball court. Fortunately no one was injured, but someone had tried to set the bleachers on fire, and several people were taken to the hospital suffering from smoke inhalation. There were none of the usual blushing brides on the pages of the *Mayfield Daily Journal* of late. No rescued puppies, nothing to touch Mrs. Billingsley's heart. The closest thing to good news she had found was the report of a five-day-old baby girl, discovered abandoned but alive on the doorstep of the Elks Hall.

Something had happened. A shift was taking place in the behavior of mankind. Mrs. Billingsley put away the dregs of her breakfast and, feeling so discouraged, considered skipping her appointment with Dr. Birnteller. But her wiser self knew this change of outlook needed psychological scrutinizing. These aberrations of the human spirit and behavior patterns weighed heavily upon her. She couldn't even muster a little interest in fashion sense or grooming and, dispensing with makeup, put on her dungarees and a brown wool sweater, which she would too late remember scratched unbearably. Mrs. Billingsley plodded out the door.

"Doctor," she began, after a moment of trying to gather her thoughts, "I am despondent." The deep depression she felt helped her let go of her fear of what the doctor would say. What could be worse than having to experience the behavior of humankind in general? She continued. "The world has disappointed me this morning in a most cruel way, and what is worse, I suspect that I must be as ordinary and flawed as the rest of humanity."

"Can you elaborate on that fear?" asked the doctor.

"You know...ordinary...brown cardigan boring. Irritating. Scratchy. I had a beautiful vision, Doctor, of mankind, and of myself as part of it. That vision has been dashed. I can no longer trust my own judgment. I look around, and surrendering my denial, really, what do I see? I live in a house with a cement front yard, for goodness' sakes. Not even crabgrass. No morning glories, no passion. I am so ordinary, I am beginning to see it now, Doctor. You have been trying to show me, and I understand now from whence have come your explosions, your attacks on me as a person. My heart aches for you, having to endure the tedium of such a patient. I feel I have just experienced an insight of such intensity that it blinds me. What am I to do?" She buried her face in her hands.

"Have you tried hang-gliding?" asked the doctor.

"I beg your pardon?"

"It's all relative, Mrs. Billingsley. I'm sorry, but your hour seems to be up."

"Would it be possible for me to use my Wednesday appointment now, Doctor?" asked Mrs. Billingsley, her lower lip trembling.

"I can only give you seventeen minutes toward Wednesday."

"That would be fine, thank you," she replied, her eyes glistening with gratitude at his generosity. "May we talk about my childhood?"

"It's your nickel. They say it's sometimes helpful."

"My childhood lasted from twelve o'clock to three one afternoon many years ago, Doctor. I've never spoken of this to anyone. I often feel that I was plucked out of time and space during my childhood and dropped into a strange and unfamiliar world. I don't know where they plucked me from, but I feel certain that if it hadn't happened, I would be a different person today. Quite taller, most probably, and definitely more accomplished. I just feel this to be true. I believe I might have become a dancer. I certainly had inclinations, but I shall never forget the painful afternoon when Elsa Blangsted had to call my mother from the Ecole de Ballet because I had gotten awkwardly stuck to the ceiling at the peak of a grand jeté. She was not even so concerned regarding my own injuries or impact with the ceiling, but rather feared what would happen when I came crashing down. She moved the entire class outdoors and conducted the remainder of the hour on the lawn, lest I fall and crush one of the other children. But the lawn had been freshly mown, and the dancers in their pink tights were soon covered with tiny particles of green grass cuttings, which made them look like hairy little green gorillas from the tutus down. I stayed stuck on the ceiling and therefore missed learning the entire first movement of the *Swan Lake* choreography. Which is why I performed so miserably later at the recital. I was literally laughed off the stage. Children do not forget these things, Doctor."

She took a moment to compose herself. The memories were flooding in painfully, though some of them didn't look familiar at all, but she went with them anyway.

"I feel I was permanently scarred. Shortly thereafter I took up the violin, and embraced the security that came with always having sheet music in front of me. There was no memorizing of choreography involved in the study of the violin. My tone, however, was unbearable, and soon my practice periods morphed into long hours of standing in the kitchen playing fingering exercises and bowing agitatedly as the cockroaches rolled onto their backs and with a final kick of their spindly little legs, gave up the ghost. Sonic pest control,

I think they call it now. If we'd had a little more serious problem with cockroaches, perhaps I would have been more valued as a child. Are my seventeen minutes up yet, Doctor?"

"No," he yawned, "but we must wrap this up. I don't have the correct change. I'll have to owe you four." And he helped Mrs. Billingsley up from the chaise and gently escorted her to the elevator.

She didn't feel much better, but she did find it interesting that she didn't feel any worse. Perhaps, she thought, therapy works when you least expect it to.

Chapter 7

Brother Goodfellow
and the Flood

Traffic had not yet thickened as Mrs. Billingsley settled in for the drive home. Her mind was reflecting on the whole process of life, or life as she was observing it in her hours with the doctor. To walk out the door of his office without feeling smaller than when she walked in was truly a sign of progress. So she must be getting better. Does one ever actually get better, she speculated, in therapy, or does the world actually get better, and so it becomes easier to function within it? Or does therapy just help you not care? Hard to know, she concluded. And really not her job.

As she headed toward the suburbs of Mayfield, a soft dusting of snow began falling on the windshield, then a heavier fall, and then wind in great gusts. A bit untimely, she thought, but was glad she had on her old brown sweater, even if it *was* scratchy. She gripped the steering wheel tightly as the windshield wipers strained against the coating of snow beginning to build up. Soon the expanse of highway before her was lined with heavy snowbanks piled along the sides of the road.

As she turned off the highway and drove closer to home, the snow had not yet been cleared off the streets of the neighborhood. Soon it became impossible to navigate, and she pulled

off the road, thinking she would leave the car in the parking
lot of the Mayfield Park Tent Theater and just try to walk
the four and a half blocks home. She circled the parking lot
several times before she finally found a spot. Irritated at the
crowded lot, she grumbled a bit as she got out, locked the
car, put on her light spring jacket, and pulled the collar up
tightly under her chin. It was freezing out and the spring
jacket didn't quite cut it in terms of keeping her warm.

Then she remembered the reason for the crowded parking lot; today was Fred Goodfellow's appearance in the Tent
Theater. Brother Goodfellow was an evangelist whose popu-
larity had soared in small towns across the country as broad-
casts of his weekly revival services went out to hundreds of
local cable stations. He wasn't her favorite man of the cloth,
but he was indeed a charismatic fellow. This Mrs. Billingsley
could not deny. She did suspect that if the truth ever came
out, it would be revealed that his dimples had been surgically
enhanced and the wavy blond hair that flowed back from his
temples kept its honeyed tones through some expensive and
very complicated dying process. But as Dr. Birnteller continually pointed out, ours is not to judge. Furthermore, it
occurred to her that *inside* his tent she would be consider-
ably warmer than standing in the parking lot *outside,* until
the snow eased up a bit. So, compromising what she considered her higher spiritual standards for the sake of avoiding
frostbite, she headed for the entrance, quietly stepped inside,
and stood at the back of the congregation.

She was amazed at the hypnotic power this preacher held
over his flock. He seemed to take control of the minds and
pocketbooks of his transfixed worshippers. Mrs. Billingsley
was not a sophisticated person, nor, in her own opinion, a
cynical one. But she was bright enough to recognize a scam
when she saw one. And here he was, this Elmer Gantry, selling his wares like proverbial hotcakes, his assistants standing at the ready with the collection baskets in hand, prepared

to walk among the crowded aisles. It was the first time she had actually been there to witness it firsthand. All along the back walls of the Tent Theater were tables piled with glossily-packaged religious products for sale, items such as inspirational books with Brother Goodfellow's smiling face on the cover, DVDs and CD recordings of his various sermons, replicas of the Last Supper painting, and something that looked like a plastic bobble-headed figure of Brother Goodfellow to bless the dashboards of the cars of his faithful followers.

The tent was full of attentive and devoted worshippers, who from time to time were moved by the spirit to raise their waving arms and shout "Amen," "Yes, Brother," and other such supportive remarks. Mrs. Billingsley, grateful as she was for the warmth of the surroundings, was finding it hard to join in the spirit. She didn't see any familiar faces in the crowd. She began to speculate about how a wise and loving God who could see through this kind of performance might handle things. She thought about the things He had pulled off in the past. There was the parting of the Red Sea, but that didn't really fit this situation since no one seemed to be trying to migrate to any place. There were the loaves and fishes. Well, Brother Goodfellow was not about to feed this crowd without a guaranteed profit margin clearly agreed upon in advance. What else was there? It had been a long time since her Bible Studies at the Ascension Lutheran Sunday School. But the crowd was getting quite caught up in the emotions of the sermon, the power of the word. The offering baskets were being passed for the second time since she had come in, and the musicians were stepping forward to begin another rousing number.

Then, she noticed what looked like water seeping under the double doors at the back of the tented area. Odd. The temperature must have changed dramatically outside to melt that much snow. Yet it was unmistakable. Suddenly the doors flung open and in washed a flood of water, sweeping the folding chairs and their occupants toward the front of the tent, picking up Brother Goodfellow, swirling him and the congregation out the other end of the tent, swooping the musicians and their instruments up as well, out into the parking lot. There wasn't time to think about what was happening or to grab hold of the tent poles. Mrs. Billingsley just tried to keep her head above the surface of the rising waters and bobbed along with the rest of the crowd. Interestingly, though there was some confusion, no one seemed to be terribly upset. Mrs. Billingsley thought perhaps most of the people presumed this was just part of the sermon, like the live-action 3-D movies growing so popular. She remembered the story about the flood and the ark, but she had a hard time envisioning all these people *and* two of every animal in the world ending up on an ark that could have found its way into Mayfield. Well, she thought, it was not her responsibility to create the storyline. On she whirled.

The torrent of water, filled now with members of the congregation trying to hold on to their handbags and their Bibles, finally letting go of their folding chairs, scanning the surface of the water for their loved ones, was rushing through the streets of Mayfield, past the snowplows, past the downtown square, past City Hall, past the Medical Building where Dr. Birnteller's office was located, rushing on and on, out through the farmlands and the fields, out past the roadways and cities dotted against the landscape. The entire world became a rolling sea, rushing forward.

"Hello, is that you, Mrs. Billingsley?" came a shout from someone floating by to her right. "Aren't Brother Goodfellow's services simply amazing?"

She turned as much as she could in the rushing torrent and saw it was the woman who worked at the local cleaners. "Hello, dear," she called back, but by then the woman had tumbled on along in front of her. One of the deacons also waved as he floated by, the contribution basket clutched tightly in his other hand, but she didn't recognize him.

In no time at all, it seemed, Mrs. Billingsley along with the entire congregation, the rest of the deacons, the handbags and Bibles, and the folding chairs were floating in the new sea that had suddenly relocated itself remarkably close to Mayfield. As the floodwaters pushed everything and everyone farther out into the waves, Mrs. Billingsley saw, looming on the horizon, a gigantic creature, a huge black whale, dramatically rising from the water, its jaws poised in a wide-open position. It occurred to her that perhaps she should alert someone to the situation, but then she remembered. It was probably all part of the plan.

On the waters rushed, and she could see that now the mouth of the giant whale was opening wider, to welcome them all in—the rush of deacons, the congregation, Brother Goodfellow, and Mrs. Billingsley herself. They tumbled in, one over the other, through the whale's jaws, through his throat and down into his belly, finally settling next to his huge liver, rather crowded and stepping on one another's toes. The space was much larger than Mrs. Billingsley had expected, and the water level seeped into the hidden corners of the whale's interior, finally leveling off to a controllable height. Everyone began to shake themselves out and settle into some kind of order, the deacons turning the chairs upright. Those few whose faith was beginning to waver started to panic; one little girl sitting next to Mrs. Billingsley was in tears.

"Don't worry, dear, this is all just part of the service, I'm quite sure..." she said, and hugged the little girl. "Where is your mommy?" But then a woman hurried over, grabbed the little girl, and went to look for a seat closer to the front of the crowd.

"Praise the Lord!" said a grey-haired gentleman standing nearby. "I wasn't none too happy about coming today. My son, you know, he's got all enthused about this Goodfellow guy, an' I always been skeptical, but I gotta tell you, I ain't *never* experienced anything like this, not in all my years as a

Christian. I'm pretty well sold!"

Mrs. Billingsley herself wasn't terribly comfortable with the situation, but tried to remain calm in order to quietly evaluate things. Brother Goodfellow, always on the lookout for an opportunity to seize focus, obviously saw this whole thing as an opportunity for strengthening faith and an affirmation of fundamentalist biblical interpretations. So he climbed up on the shoulders of two of the larger men standing near the entrance to the throat of the whale and began shouting to the crowd.

"There's no cause for concern, my beloved brothers and sisters," he cried. "You must try to remain calm and trust in the Lord...this is only a test," he assured them.

Mrs. Billingsley didn't think he looked at all that sure about it himself, but it did seem to be calming his followers a bit.

Brother Goodfellow continued, promising them with convincing and pastoral fervor that deliverance was imminent, and furthermore, since he was apparently never one to waste a captive audience, that there would soon again be a steady Republican hand at the helm in Washington, D.C.

"Deacons," he instructed, "pass the baskets!" And then to the congregation, "Reach deeply into your pockets, my friends...salvation is at hand. Show the Lord we are grateful for his watchful eye! He is sharing with us the gift of experiencing the truths of His word, of the living Bible, here and now. Praise Him! Show your thanks, brave children of the Lord!"

And the deacons made their way with the soggy collection baskets through the increasingly agitated crowd, sloshing in water up to their knees.

Then Brother Goodfellow began to lead them in the singing of a hymn. "Shall...we...gather...at...the...ri...ver..." he sang. But he too late realized his unfortunate choice of material. Their voices had at first risen in trembling, passionate tones that echoed against the whale's solar plexus, but began to falter the minute they got to the part about the river. The irony seemed to cast a pall over the crowd. Their joyous, ringing voices quickly died down and they began to grow angrier and more rebellious.

Dinnertime was approaching, and empty stomachs rumbled, the only full stomach being that of the whale's. The evangelist soon realized he was losing control when his flock began to rush at him, pummeling him with their Bibles, and fighting one another for optimum positions that might allow them access to air and an occasional peek out through the whale's mouth. Perhaps, he realized, they were not ready for this close connection with the Holy Spirit.

Eventually the vibrations caused by the milling about of all the angry, hungry worshippers began to cause the whale to have extreme indigestion. The sides of his stomach rippled in a reflex reaction, his body's effort to eject the offending foreign objects, and the crowd again began to be tossed and swirled about, the ripples moving them closer and closer to the opening of the whale's throat. Brother Goodfellow saw what was happening and frantically tried to formulate a brief sermon claiming credit for the release of the crowds from their imprisonment, saying that the Lord was delivering them.

"You see, the Lord has heard our prayers, as He always does when we tithe appropriately! Redemption is at hand... do not be afraid, my brothers and sisters!"

Mrs. Billingsley tried to allow the older congregants to tumble on past her, and any children that had also gotten swept into the whale. *We have a responsibility to look out for one another,* she felt, *even if no one looks out for us.* This was not something Brother Goodfellow talked much about, but she always remembered it from Ascension Lutheran Bible Studies.

Soon most of the congregation had pretty much been

swept out through the jaws, save for a few hearty souls who were reluctant to leave the reverend's side. She could see one of the deacons huddled with him, both of them speaking intensely now in energetic tones. Then Brother Goodfellow patted his colleague on the back, took a pad and pen out of his coat pocket, and began to scribble something frantically. The whale's interior was nearly empty now, save for Brother Goodfellow, the deacon beside him, one other worshipper whose jacket had gotten caught on one of the whale's back teeth, and Mrs. Billingsley. The spasmodic stomach ripples began to ease a bit. The deacon grabbed the pad from Brother Goodfellow and tried to hand it to the last worshipper, untangling him from the whale's tooth. But once the man was loose, he somersaulted on by, and soon was out of reach. They looked around desperately, and then spotted Mrs. Billingsley.

"Dear madam," Brother Goodfellow shouted, realizing she was the last person remaining, save the deacon and himself. "A divine thought has just occurred to us. Why not broadcast the revival service right from this spot, right from the belly of the whale? We've written a note to the network proposing the plan, but we must get it out safely. Please, dear lady, can you deliver it for us?" They both now were clinging to the whale's tonsil, resisting the propelling motion that was sweeping past them.

It *was* somewhat a stroke of brilliance, Mrs. Billingsley had to admit. Surely they would be the first to accomplish such original programming. The lighting would perhaps be a problem and they would have to negotiate with the whale in order to get the necessary cables and seating in place. Perhaps they could even arrange for a world tour...the whale could travel from continent to continent...well, maybe they'd best skip Japan. They could broadcast remotely, and it could be but one in a series of "Actual Bible Stories Recreated in Their Original Settings." The whale was an act that would be tough to follow, of course, but there was the Red Sea thing, a possible ratings grabber, and eventually, of course, they'd need to put a heavier emphasis on the New Testament. The series could end with the Resurrection, or perhaps the Rapture, which would of course inspire a repeat of all the previous episodes. Yes, it was brilliant, she had to admit.

Mrs. Billingsley realized she'd better act fast or risk becoming a permanent fixture inside the whale, so she grabbed the note from the reverend's hand and waved goodbye as the final reflexive thrust of the whale's belly carried her out through the jaws and suddenly and miraculously deposited her into the parking lot of the Mayfield Tent Theater. She landed with a thud, a bit shaken at first, but fortunately the snow was still deep enough that it cushioned her landing and she experienced no serious injury.

She shook herself free of the residual saltwater drippings, found her car among the crowded lot, and managed to get back onto the road. She turned on the heater, cranked up the defogger, and stuffed Brother Goodfellow's note into the pocket of her spring jacket, which was also still dripping with salt water but drying reasonably quickly thanks to the warm air now flowing into the interior of the car.

The road had cleared enough that she was able to make good progress toward home. She thought about Brother Goodfellow and the deacon, there in the belly of the whale, joyfully anticipating the next exciting level of their ministry, reporting from the original biblical sites the miraculous stories from both the Old and the New Testaments. It was impressive; she had to admit. But at best, it would be a while before the network heads could agree on this new proposal, as you really had to have been there. Brother Goodfellow and his friend would have to survive on the undigested bits of octopus and shark floating around in the confines of their new studio. They would probably lose a few pounds waiting for the network crew to show up, she thought, which could only improve their on-screen appeal. She would have to find a way to get his note to the gentlemen at the Christian Broadcasting Network as soon as possible, despite her lack of enthusiasm for the good brother and his crew.

But wait, she thought. If this *was* truly a divine inspiration, the idea would surely have occurred to the network heads and Brother Goodfellow simultaneously. They would think of it, with or without the note from Brother Goodfellow. The light of truth would illuminate at once all beings of faith, and they were probably already on their way to the whale with the crew. This might just be an opportunity for an excellent testament of faith.

Mrs. Billingsley reached into her pocket and pulled out Brother Goodfellow's note. She rolled the car window down just enough to reach her hand out and send the note floating into the whirling, tossing snow. She watched it dance up into the wind, sweep off into the distance, and gradually drift out of sight. She experienced a brief moment of remorse in light of the possibility that she might have just interfered with divine destiny. But the moment passed quickly, and she smiled, anticipating the ease with which she might be able to find a parking place at the Tent Theater next time she got stuck in a snowstorm during the Revival Meeting season.

Chapter 8

the Fish Scale *and the* Knight *in* Shining Armor

It was nearly four in the morning. Mrs. Billingsley paced the linoleum floor of her kitchen. She could not quiet her mind. Things had been going so well at the doctor's, and her subconscious mind, she felt, was making great progress. But her conscious mind was troubled, and she could not shake this sleeplessness. She was worried about Mr. Billingsley.

For weeks now he had been behaving strangely, very unlike himself. He had taken to stopping every afternoon at the Cat & Fiddle Saloon and Fish House after work. Swearing he was having only one Gulden Draak dark ale and a side order of deep-fried cod, he kept assuring her that everything was fine and that the stresses of business had compounded to necessitate this unwinding on the way home, and that she absolutely should not worry.

But she absolutely *was* worrying. Mr. Billingsley was growing larger and larger. She was certain he was consuming more than just a side order and one Gulden Draak, and furthermore, she had occasionally detected what appeared to be faint lipstick traces on the increasingly tight collars of his dress shirts. This behavior was truly unlike him. She was frightened and determined to ask the doctor's advice that morning. Her confidence in Dr. Birnteller was growing daily, and she felt certain he would be able to guide her through this stormy sea.

She finished her warm milk and returned to bed to try to sleep the two remaining hours before Mr. Billingsley's alarm went off. As she hung her robe on the bathroom door, something caught her eye. Silvery, iridescent—she thought Mr. Billingsley might have dropped one of his contact lenses on the tile floor. She stooped to retrieve it and stood for a moment, puzzling over what the object might be. Not a lens, as she had thought. Not a piece of broken glass...much too smooth and light. Then she realized what it was. She had seen dozens of them on the fishing trip she and Mr. Billingsley had taken on the West Coast several years ago. The inside of the ship's floor was covered with these delicate, shiny objects. They were fish scales.

Once she finally admitted to herself what the object was, she also had to admit that this was not the first one she had seen recently. There had been several on the bathroom floor where Mr. Billingsley stepped out of the shower to dry. They looked like droplets of water, and yet they were still there later in the afternoon when she vacuumed.

Mrs. Billingsley wrapped the tiny scale carefully in a piece of tissue and put it in the side pocket of her purse to show the doctor. It was physical proof that something very out of the ordinary was occurring.

The alarm rang at six o'clock. Mr. Billingsley was already up and in the shower. Mrs. Billingsley went downstairs to make coffee. She brought in the paper and set the table. She pressed his blue Brooks Brothers button-down collared shirt. Still no sign of him. She wrote out instructions for the cleaning lady and read the food section of the *Mayfield Tribune*. She whipped up a batch of whole-grain waffles and poured herself a third cup of coffee. It was now eight-fifteen. Something was not right. She filled Mr. Billingsley's favorite mug with coffee and carried it upstairs. Through the bathroom door she could hear the shower still running. She stepped inside the bathroom and tapped lightly on the shower door.

"Dear," she said gently, "it's nearly eight-thirty. You won't have time for breakfast. I've brought your coffee."

"Thank you, Naomi... Just give me a hand, would you, through the door here. I'm afraid it's gotten a bit tight."

Mr. Billingsley turned off the shower and opened the door, extending a chubby hand to her. She gave a tug, and out he popped. She really hadn't noticed that his girth had reached such an alarming proportion. Definitely something had to be done, and soon. Fortunately, her regularly scheduled appointment with the doctor was today at ten o'clock.

Soon Mr. Billingsley came downstairs, the collar of his Brooks Brothers shirt straining a bit but obviously still buttonable. He grabbed his briefcase, kissed her on the cheek, and headed for the front door.

"Dear," she called after him, "I've reserved your copy of *Captain from Castile* at the video store...do hurry home, won't you?"

"Wonderful, my sweet," he exclaimed, and promised that he would make only a quick stop at the Cat & Fiddle and come right home. Last week it had taken *Mutiny on the Bounty* to lure him back in time for supper, and before that, two Errol Flynn pirate movies. Mr. Billingsley had developed an insatiable craving for anything to do with the sea, and Netflix was batting a thousand. But she shuddered at the thought that one day there would be no more seafaring tales, and then she might lose him forever.

Traffic was particularly heavy as Mrs. Billingsley made her way into town. Not wanting to waste more time looking for a parking place, she pulled into the underground parking area and took the elevator directly to the seventh floor. She was confident the doctor would help her find a solution.

And indeed, the doctor was at the ready. He met her at the door of the office astride a white steed, wearing a suit of armor. Mrs. Billingsley had to put on her sunglasses, the glare from the polished metal was so bright. She immediately felt a sense of relief and confidence that this situation *would* be handled, and swiftly. But she was compelled to suggest that he might be more comfortable during their hour if he sat in his Eames chair rather than remaining on the horse.

"Don't be concerned, Mrs. Billingsley. I find this affords a helpful overview. Sometimes we get too close to the problem to be effective therapeutically. Let us get started."

"Very well." She looked up at him intently. "You see, I know this is more a conscious problem than an unconscious one, but I am so worried about Mr. Billingsley. He has taken to stuffing himself every afternoon with cod and dark ale on his way home from work, his morning showers have taken on oceanic proportions, he is growing larger by the day, and last night I found *this* on the floor of the bathroom."

She produced the fish scale from her handbag and handed it up to the doctor, who steadied the horse while he made a closer examination of the object.

"Mrs. Billingsley, you were absolutely correct in bringing this to me. We have a matter of gravest severity. I believe this is indicative of a newly discovered and very rare emotional disorder...in layman's terms, a kind of genetic distortion, a kink in time, so to speak. The genes of the patient begin to respond to subconscious genetically-stored information, and the patient becomes enslaved by a sort of compulsive behavior pattern not his own. We must first explore the possibility of his having some sort of ancestral history with the sea. Do you have any recollection of Mr. Billingsley's family being a seafaring lot?"

"Well, now that you mention it, Doctor, his family was from Wales originally, and I believe they were men of the sea. I recall a bizarre tale he told me once about a distant ancestor who sailed the high seas and had a weakness for dark ale and wild women. The fellow died at sea, in fact, in a rather unfortunate accident."

"Aha. I believe we are on the trail of something. Can you elaborate on the accident?"

"Well, it's rather embarrassing, Doctor, but if you feel it is important. The poor devil consumed an inordinate amount of ale...all they had on board, I believe, and broke his neck in a fall."

"He slipped on the deck, Mrs. Billingsley?"

"No, Doctor, not exactly. He, well...he fell into the sea during a storm, after an unsuccessful attempt at penetrating the voluptuous carving on the bow of the ship. Apparently they had been at sea for some time, and he'd rather gone 'round the bend even before the ale incident."

"Mrs. Billingsley, I think we've found the right genetic memory culprit. But we can handle this, if we've caught it in time. If I may offer some suggestions, the first step is that you must begin heavily over-salting his food. He will not notice it at first, but a certain subtle aversion therapy will be taking place. Deep within his genes, part of him is longing to return to the sea. We must shatter this genetic hope before he is driven to bring it to full fruition."

Mrs. Billingsley shuddered at the ominous prospect before her. To lose Mr. Billingsley to the briny deep just when it was beginning to feel like their relationship was really getting on track, at least in her subconscious, would indeed be tragic.

"I'll start immediately, Doctor. Have you any other thoughts?"

"Yes, put away all the large bath sheets, so he will have to dry off with hand towels. There will be an annoying experience of not being able to get sufficiently dry. You might also add some sea salt to your hot water heater. And sprinkle some sand over the floor on his side of the bed. It will be difficult for you as well, Mrs. Billingsley, but sacrifices must be made. Other things may occur to you on a subconscious level. Go with your instincts."

The doctor backed the horse away from the door and allowed Mrs. Billingsley to pass, wishing her the best of luck as he flipped the visor on his helmet back into place.

Chapter 9

Lunch *at the* Cat & Fiddle Pub

Mrs. Billingsley felt encouraged by the doctor's advice and was determined to put the plan into action. She would work out some of the details over lunch, and considered stopping at the Mayfield Tea Room for finger sandwiches and ambrosia salad, but then a better thought occurred to her. Why not have lunch at the Cat & Fiddle? She could evaluate the enemy on its own turf. She retrieved her car from Parking Level 2 and, emboldened by Dr. Birnteller's words, hurried down the parkway toward the pub.

Outside the entrance, she steeled herself. This was hostile territory, and she had no idea what awaited her. She stepped inside and waited for a moment while her eyes adjusted to the darkened room. The place was quite crowded. Two waitresses dressed in wench costumes, low cut at both ends, and wearing fishnet hose and spiked heels were on duty. One leaned against the bar, touching up her lipstick as she waited for a drink order, and another delivered a huge tray of fish and chips to one of the tables along the side of the room. Two men were playing darts at the rear of the table area. There was a large blackboard behind the bar with daily specials listed, and the room was filled with male customers who were, to a man, on the round side. *How widespread this seems to have become*, she thought. *Oh my goodness, another subconscious insight*. Also behind the bar was a huge aquarium filled with large and colorful fish, and on the sandy bottom of the aquarium sat a miniature wreck of an ancient pirate ship. Treasures were strewn about on its hull, spilling over onto the sandy bottom of the aquarium. And the piped-in music, though the level was low and not at all intrusive, was definitely a collection of jaunty pirate melodies, to which the male diners were inconspicuously swaying to and fro in meter, and raising their glasses of ale.

Mrs. Billingsley felt out of place. She had put on her navy gabardine pants suit that morning and carried her very good copy of a Chanel handbag. A smallish blue hat with a jaunty white band completed what she now fervently hoped might be mistaken for a nautical theme. Her forehead wound had by now healed beautifully, so she no longer needed the veil. The male customers seemed not to notice her arrival, but both of the waitresses eyed her suspiciously as she moved bravely toward the bar and settled onto a barstool. She sat primly, handbag in her lap, studying the menu. A rather wizened old fellow with a droopy mustache and a neck kerchief busied himself behind the bar. With what seemed like deliberately slow movements, he finally abandoned his glass-polishing activities and approached her.

"What'll it be, ma'am?"

Thinking she was seated at a bar and should order something alcoholic to fit in with the crowd, she asked, "Do you make a Pink Squirrel, please?" as assertively as she could manage.

"We got ales, beers, soft drinks, clam broth, buttermilk, and lo-fat, lady. No Pink Squirrels."

"I'll have a light beer, please, and the Fisherman's Daily Special."

"Right y'are." And he reached down below the bar for a beer, pouring it with a flourish into one of the freshly polished glasses. Beer was not Mrs. Billingsley's drink. But she was a woman on a mission. She sipped slowly, watching the fish in the tank floating back and forth. She noticed two strangely marked fish, and upon closer scrutiny realized they appeared to have little suits on, and tiny wing-tipped shoes at the ends of their fins. She shuddered and slowly turned away from the bar.

She tried to look into the faces of the customers without appearing obvious. They had smiles on their faces, most of them, and they wore tranquil, almost glazed expressions. Occasionally a waitress would lean over one of them as she set a steaming plate of food down before them and gave them a kiss on the cheek and a pat on the head. They were either responding to the attention, happily stuffed and feeling the narcotic effects of overeating, or someone was spiking their tartar sauce.

But the men seemed mannerly. They just seemed to be in some kind of a mental fog. Could it be they suffered from the same affliction as Mr. Billingsley? There was something insidious going on here, and the tragic part was that it was all perfectly legal. There were no laws against over-nauticalization. There were no laws against fish wearing wing tips. There were no laws against large men gathering in dark places for salty lunches served by friendly waitresses. It was all perfectly legal. Yet these men all, most likely, had homes and families away from whom they were slipping little by little, day by day, one knot at a time. Could it really be they all somehow suffered from the same genetic compulsive disorder that Mr. Billingsley had inherited? Could it be they all had family histories that dated back to men of the sea? Very strange, she thought, but how else could all this be explained? She would have to report back to Dr. Birnteller that there appeared to be an epidemic. And this pub seemed to be making a fortune on it.

Mrs. Billingsley tried to engage the man behind the bar in conversation as she waited for her order, hoping to draw out of him some revealing clues about what exactly went on behind the veil of the Cat & Fiddle.

"You have quite a lunch crowd today, I notice...are these all your regular customers, sir?"

"Yes ma'am. Seems like our regulars just can't get enough of us. We had to extend our lunch hours to three-thirty, then to four o'clock. Just couldn't get some o' these fellas to go home. I don't know what the cook puts in that chowder, but it sure keeps 'em comin' back!"

"Yes, I can see that. Dressed quite formally too, some of them...professional men, most of them, suits and wing tips—definitely come right from the office, don't they?"

"Guess so, ma'am." He seemed anxious to change the subject. "Here's your order, nice and hot..."

He produced a bowl of steamy white clam chowder and a basket of crusty French bread, accompanied by two squares of cheese. Mrs. Billingsley tried the chowder. Its flavor, the delicate seasonings, the smell of the sea wafting up from its steam, washed over her with the first spoonful. She ignored the cheese and the bread, her usual weakness. She ignored the light beer. She finished off the first bowl and ordered a second. She felt the waistband of her gabardine slacks growing tighter. She could not put down her spoon. So this was what it was like. This was the demon with which Mr. Billingsley wrestled. And she hadn't even ordered the English Ale. She knew she had to break the spell.

"Please, sir, bring me the bill and a dish of chocolate ice cream."

"No ice cream, lady. Only saltwater taffy, and our special Deep Sea Steaming Latte Frothe."

Mrs. Billingsley knew she was in over her head. Calmly, she reached into her bag and withdrew two twenty-dollar bills. With a steely gaze, she said to the barman, "Keep the change." She rose from her barstool, walked through the middle of the room, past the large, nodding, smiling men, and out the door of the pub. Once more in the sunshine, she could see truly what a close call it had been. She had underestimated the power of the enemy. This would require all the strength and dedication she could muster. She drove home to prepare for battle.

Several weeks had passed since Mrs. Billingsley's conversation with the doctor and her visit to the Cat & Fiddle. Things seemed to be going well. She had carefully been following the doctor's advice, beginning with the over-salting of Mr. Billingsley's food. And he had begun to react to this. Not quite as quickly as Mrs. Billingsley had hoped, but at least there was a reaction. The doctor encouraged her to have patience, to stay with the program. While the last moments of her dinner preparations were simmering on the stove, Mrs. Billingsley took out a load of hand towels from the washing machine and placed them in the dryer. Mr. Billingsley hadn't found the supply of bath sheets hidden behind the vacuum cleaner in the front hall closet, and he had been coming down to breakfast every morning in ill humor, his damp dress shirt sticking to the back of the kitchen chair. And Mrs. Billingsley noticed he'd been leaving more of his oatmeal uneaten in the bowl as she'd increased the amount of salt. So something was working. A week had passed since she'd found any fish scales on the bathroom floor, and two weeks since Mr. Billingsley had needed help ejecting himself from the shower. He hadn't seemed to notice anything out of the ordinary about the sand on the floor next to his bed, but he did seem a bit out of sorts when he had to brush off the bottoms of his feet before pulling the covers up. His boss at Bumble Bee Pharmaceuticals, Mr. O'Mally, had cooperated with her requests by keeping him at the office late each night, so there was only time for a quick glass of ale at the Cat & Fiddle on the way home, and on some days he didn't even stop at all. All of it seemed to be coming together to interrupt the genetic fixation that was creating this magnetic force pulling him toward the sea. The night before, he had even fallen asleep during *Robin Hood and the Pirates* on the Turner Classic Movies Channel. The tide seemed to be quietly drifting away.

Finally, on this Monday night of the fifth week of the new regime, Mr. Billingsley picked up his plate of ground sirloin with anchovy sauce and threw it on the floor, knocking over his salt-rimmed margarita glass in the process.

"What's happening to me?" he cried in an anguished tone. "Please, please, Naomi, bring me some plain mashed potatoes and steamed cauliflower. No seasoning, no whimsical coloring or shapes to distract me. And please, may I have some plain room-temperature distilled water, no ice, and may I have it in my 'I LOVE NY' mug?"

Mrs. Billingsley smiled. She went to the kitchen and took the frozen mashed potatoes from the freezer. She had prepared for this day. She placed the potatoes in the microwave and slipped the cauliflower into the boiling water. She gratefully picked up the fragments of broken china and glass, ground sirloin, and anchovy sauce from the linoleum, wiped the floor clean, and threw the last of her carefully prepared over-salted cuisine in the trash. Then she tenderly dished up the mashed potatoes and cauliflower and placed the food on a milk-white plate with some fresh salt-free silverware.

When she returned to the dining room, Mr. Billingsley was sitting with his head on his arms, leaning over the table, sobbing. Salty tears spilled onto his placemat. She put the plate of food down and held him, stroking his hair softly. He seemed so bereft that it took all the strength she had to refrain from offering him a quick fix of salted nuts or a handful of Fritos. The truly loving thing to do does not always seem the kindest, in the moment of decision.

He sat up, wiped the tears away with the back of his slightly less chubby hand, and in doing so, got a bit of the salty tears on his lips. As soon as he tasted the tears, a flood of understanding rushed over him.

"My God, Naomi, it's been inside me all the while. This craving, this searching, this insatiable quest that nearly drove me to the edge. I had it all the time. I should have been looking inside. I'm as salty a bastard as I could ever hope to become. And you stuck by me through all of it. I'm so ashamed. I'm going to pay off my tab at the Cat & Fiddle, throw away my wing tips, and start to live again."

Mrs. Billingsley wiped a tear from her own eye. She was a pretty salty old girl herself. She sat down next to him and shared a bit of his unsalted mashed potatoes. Gratefully, she realized it. They had *both* come a long way.

Chapter 10

a More Romantic Life Through Landscaping

Sunlight poured through the kitchen windows as Mrs. Billingsley joyously set about preparing breakfast. Her heart this day was filled with anticipation, because she had conceived of a plan that so delighted her she could barely wait to get it underway. She rejoiced at the recent healing that had taken place—the dark days of Mr. Billingsley's genetic sea fixation were gone, and the residual symptoms would correct themselves, she was certain, with time. Her instinctive wisdom and courage, which seemed to be blossoming of late, had found affirmation in the success of her efforts...fully acknowledging, of course, Dr. Birnteller's help. But Mrs. Billingsley realized that one cannot be too watchful. She guessed that even the professionals could be caught asleep at the marriage wheel. And she had determined that her own relationship would do well, now that it seemed back on track, with a little revitalizing. She felt encouraged to once again trust her instincts. She was going to take a more active role in shaping her own marital landscape. She was about to take another risk.

It was the morning of Mr. Billingsley's departure for the Pharmaceutical Suppliers Convention in Peoria. He would be gone for at least six or seven days, which, if she worked fast enough, would be sufficient time. As soon as he had finished his breakfast and was off to the airport, she whirled into action.

First she called Mac Gregor Demolition, and after settling on what she considered a fair price for their willingness to schedule immediately, she arranged for them to tear up the recently-concreted front yard and remove all the chunks by the end of the workday. She understood that Mr. Billingsley had chosen to have this work done for what he considered the best of reasons—practicality of maintenance, reduction of gardening fees, conservation of water use. However, she had to trust that once her project was complete, he would adjust to the changes and realize on all levels the wisdom of her decision.

She then called Mayfield Hills Nursery and Garden Supply and gave them a list of plants and flowers she had carefully prepared, most of which they fortunately had in stock. Next, she contacted Clark Electric and Plumbing and explained her needs and the urgency thereof. They agreed to come first thing the next morning to begin the necessary installations. Her order at Tropical Aviary Imports was a little more complicated, but arrangements were nonetheless put into place. Several of her requests would have to be specially ordered from the Exotic Sacred Guardians Pet Importers in Chicago and shipped by air. But Mrs. Billingsley was quite willing to cover the additional costs.

Soon the Mac Gregor crew was in the front yard with their heavy equipment, hammering at the concrete and then scooping it up in the big arms of their prehistoric-looking machine, loading the pieces into the huge truck and hauling it off to the dump.

Mrs. Billingsley stopped off at the nursery with a diagram of the yard, indicating where she wished the planting and landscaping placed.

Then it was time to address her own personal landscaping. She drove down to Murphy's Department Store, second-floor Women's Wear, and found a wonderful peasant skirt with yards of brightly colored cotton, the skirt drawn up on one side of the front and secured with a glittery rose, which allowed her to reveal a length of rather well-preserved Billingsley leg. To wear with it, she selected an off-the-shoulder white peasant blouse trimmed with an earthy cotton lace. Some black ankle-strap heels and a pair of large hoop earrings completed the look. She already had a drawer full of bangle bracelets at home left over from the seventies.

By the end of day one, the concrete was gone, the dust had settled, and Mrs. Billingsley sensed that enormous progress had already been made. In the morning, the crew from Clark Electric and Plumbing set about their work, laying pipes, carefully installing the necessary wiring. Things were moving along splendidly. Mr. Clark's brother-in-law, Elmer Franklyn, did wonderful carpentry work, and she explained to him at the end of day two what she wanted done with the front porch, after all the piping was laid and connected to the main water line. He showed up the next morning with his tools, a plentiful supply of wood, white paint to match the trim on the front door and window frames, and the special carved pieces Mrs. Billingsley had requested for the porch railing.

On day three, while the gardening crew of Mayfield Hills Nursery and Garden Supply worked their magic, Mrs. Billingsley stopped by the outdoor furniture department at Murphy's and selected several pieces she felt would add the requisite charm and ambiance to the front porch in its newly conceived state. They were promised for next-day delivery. She returned home just in time to greet the gentleman from the electronics department, with whom she had worked out the sound design for the garden.

On the fourth day, while the gardening crews took care of the finishing touches, Mrs. Billingsley went to work on a little magic of her own. She booked a facial, a manicure and pedicure, a hair weaving, and a Scandinavian body wrap. She chose to patronize the upscale day spa at the Mayfair

Downtown Hilton Inn, which was a luxury she seldom afforded herself, but this was toward a very special end.

By the sixth day, everything was perfect. Mrs. Billingsley would be home just in time for the twilight cocktail hour. Mrs. Billingsley brought the pina colada mix and Jamaican rum in from the front porch where Al's Liquor Store delivery had left it. As she floated gracefully through the house, she heard the music of the banana boats in the primitive reachings of her mind. She dressed, generously dabbing Jungle Gardenia in the crooks of her elbows, behind her knees, and on the white curves of her shoulders, which peeked out above the lace neckline of the peasant blouse. She mixed a batch of pina coladas and went to the front yard to wait for Mr. Billingsley on what used to be the front porch. It was now transformed into a veranda, the likes of which would have made Sadie Thompson proud. White curved posts held the railing in place, potted palms stood in the corners, and vines curved up along the bottom of the railings from the newly planted gardens below.

The yard was a tropical paradise. Palm trees and huge ferns hovered around little paths that wound through the yard from the driveway. Orchids bloomed in pots beneath the trees. Plumeria blossoms scented the air, and hibiscus bushes in full bloom stretched along the front of the veranda. It was remarkable what the nursery had been able to accomplish in just a few days.

And strung from the roof, out across the yard, were delicate paper lanterns containing low-wattage lights that glowed softly. The sensuous sound of steel drums floated from the distance and soft guitar music filled the garden, all from carefully hidden speakers tucked behind tree trunks and underneath ferns. On the veranda, a wicker swing hung suspended from the ceiling on two long chains. A small, round table and two wicker chairs stood at one end of the veranda and several brightly colored birds sat preening themselves on the porch railing. A huge creature with bright blue feathers and yellows, reds, and greens in its tail plumage sat in a tall cage at the bottom of the stairs, moving its head and large, hooked beak from side to side as if it was a sentry prepared to pass judgment on all those who would enter.

Mrs. Billingsley turned the newly installed handle by the sprinkler controls, and soft mist began to fall across the garden. It spattered on the roof of the veranda and dripped from the pointed tips of the palm leaves. It glistened on the paths and on the white paint of the veranda railing. It pitter-pattered on the huge blue bird, which spread its tail feathers, threw back its head, and shook its body, sending the cool drops flying in all directions.

Through the foliage, Mrs. Billingsley watched the headlights of a car approach and turn into the driveway. It paused for a moment with the motor running, just at the entrance, then started to back out of the driveway and into the street again. But then it stopped at the edge of the street and once more cautiously, slowly drove back up the driveway toward the house and parked. A silhouetted form stepped out of the car and moved toward the palms, stepped back out of sight for a moment, and then reappeared, carrying an umbrella.

Mrs. Billingsley smiled as she watched Mr. Billingsley come down the winding path and into the soft glow of the hanging lanterns. He loosened his tie, removed his suit coat, and threw it over one shoulder, foreign-correspondent-style. He was eyeing her from beneath the umbrella. He looked a little confused, but not unhappy.

"Come, darling," Mrs. Billingsley purred, "I have pina coladas and soft music, and I have sweet pineapple and black beans with rice, and smiling little fish waiting for you to bite their tails off. I have soft breezes and a full moon. Thousands of miles away, the great glacier has shaken at its core, melting its icy shores and sending its ripples to the evening star and beyond. We are part of it all, and a miraculous transformation surrounds us. The steel drums in the distance signal a new beginning. There will be no more concrete front yards for us, no more outdoor carpeting in the garage. There will be insect bites and hangovers, perhaps...but it will be because we have sought them out, not because we were defenseless against them."

Mr. Billingsley stepped up onto the veranda, dropping the umbrella behind him on the misty lawn. He smiled at Mrs. Billingsley, tossed his jacket over one of the chairs, and refilled her pina colada glass from the icy, chilled crystal pitcher on the little round table.

Then he kissed her just above the collarbone and bit the tail off one of the smiling fish.

Chapter 11

the Doctor Takes *a* Tumble

Mrs. Billingsley was early for her appointment. Eager to report to the doctor the happy results of her enthusiastic application of his very helpful suggestions, she flipped absentmindedly through the pages of an old *PEOPLE* magazine, keeping one eye on the clock. Then she moved on to Condé Nast's *Traveler*. But it was now ten minutes *past* the hour. Had she come on the wrong day? She couldn't very well interrupt the doctor if he was with another patient, but maybe if she flipped the red waiting light again, he would notice and come to investigate. She did so and sat back down to finish an article about bicycle touring along the canals of Holland.

Ten more minutes went by. Perhaps the doctor had such a boring patient this morning that he drifted off and didn't notice the red light. She would be doing all three of them a favor if she lightly knocked on the door and refocused his attention.

Tap, tap, tap.

Silence. Tap, tap, tap a little more firmly. Nothing.

What if, God forbid, the doctor and his patient had gotten into a battle of the psyches and had managed to wound each other critically? She envisioned them both spent, lying on the carpet, chests heaving, gasping for air, too weak to call for help.

This is ridiculous, she thought. *Put on our flak jackets. We're going in.*

She opened the door to the inner office. At first it looked like the room was empty, but then the doctor's chair spun slowly around to face her. Mrs. Billingsley was alarmed. He didn't look at all like himself.

"Hello, Mrs. Billingsley. I was hoping you would just go away. But I can see that's not an option for you. Why don't we just agree that this is not a canceled appointment and you don't have to pay for it, but we'll just pretend all this never happened."

"All what, Doctor?" She was beginning to be concerned.

"This...this stupid relationship between two people who pretend to care about each other...you, who pretend to respect my skills as a practitioner of mental health, and I, who pretend to have them."

Mrs. Billingsley studied him in the dim light. His face was drawn and his eyes were bloodshot and rimmed with red. He had drawn the shades down, and his desk lamp was not lit. Maybe this was simply eyestrain from reading his psychiatric journals. That would make a person grumpy, wouldn't it? But his nose was red, and his hands were shaking. And his usual attire of navy business suit, bow tie, and brown loafers had been replaced by wrinkled grey running sweats and dirty sneakers.

She gathered her courage once more. This was not right. Obviously, this morning their focus needed to be on Dr. Birnteller. She wouldn't bore him with compliments or expressions of gratitude for his fine work, or a report on how well things were going at home. She would just let *him* talk, as he had let *her* so many mornings.

"Doctor, is there something you'd like to tell me...is there something troubling you today?"

"I just told you, Mrs. Billingsley. You really don't need a psychiatrist, you're just part of what covers my overhead. Besides, I'm way off my game. I can't even run my own life, let alone yours. Just leave me here, please..."

This was rather ironic. She hadn't been that far wrong in her speculations in the waiting room. But it was his *own* psyche the doctor had been doing battle with, and obviously it was badly wounded. It lay on the Berber carpet, bleeding, next to a pile of used Kleenex issues.

"There, there, Doctor...why don't we just use the rest of my hour and try to talk this out? I have plenty of time. It's no imposition at all. I understand about the doctor-patient confidentiality, and I give you my word this will be absolutely between us. Just take a deep breath...that's it...there, now, try to tell me what's upset you so!"

The doctor took a tissue and blew his nose, then tossed it onto the pile at his feet. He lifted his eyes painfully and faced her.

"This is very...very difficult...for me to talk about."

"Just begin at the beginning, or in the middle, if it's easier. We'll put the pieces together later."

"Well, Mrs. Bill...uh, may I call you Naomi?"

"Of course, Doctor. You may call me anything you like."

"Well, Naomi, my wife is a very lovely woman. Of course, I don't talk about her here because it's...well, it's not the kind of thing you talk about with your patients. We have been married eleven years, and like everyone else, we've had our little ups and downs. But I always thought I handled things pretty well. When she gets upset, I always remind her that it is not events themselves, but one's perception of them, that is distressing. Usually that settles her and seems to turn things around. Occasionally I admit, if I become extremely frustrated with her behavior, I have in the past disappointed myself by losing my patience."

"You...let me try to be delicate, Doctor...you don't ever become physical with her, do you?"

"Oh God, no, I just flare my nostrils a little bit, or find that a good glare usually turns things around. Sometimes I have to send her to her room for a 'time out,' but she most always bounces back cheerfully. I believe in rewarding good behavior, Naomi, and I try to remember to send a Hallmark card periodically. She has her own charge account at Mayfair Village Market, I acknowledged our anniversary last month with a new Waring Blender, top of the line model with the ice crusher attachment...we vacationed at the Sheraton Pittsburgh last spring when I was asked to speak at the Mental Hygiene Convention...we even had room service...I...I just..."

His voice broke, and his shoulders shook uncontrollably.

Mrs. Billingsley pondered as to which psychological tack to take. She had never been on this side of the wall before. There really wasn't enough time left in her hour, it seemed, to get Freudian. Perhaps just a direct dose of Behavioral could straighten things out. But it did need an emergency shot of something pretty powerful.

"It seems to me that this is fixable, Doctor. Perhaps if we could get the two of you together here during my next appointment..."

"No, you don't understand. When I got home last night, there were three places set at the table. My wife didn't even offer me my customary scotch and water. She didn't have the newspaper and my slippers set next to my leather chair. She was dressed in a dress I've never seen before...somewhat overly revealing but not entirely unattractive. She had—what is that stuff women wear sometimes, Mrs. Billingsley, eye outliner? And she had perfume on. I thought at first that she'd just forgotten about my allergies, but we've certainly talked about that often enough. I'm inclined to think it was a blatant act of rebellion. And she—*she*—had a drink in her hand."

"Maybe she'd just had a hard day", she suggested. "Women sometimes do, you know..."

"No, no. Let me finish...I went into the kitchen to fix myself my scotch and water, and when I walked back into the living room, there was a man sitting next to my wife on the sofa. My wife said to me, 'This is Armando,' and the fellow actually got up, came over, and shook my hand."

"Well now, it really would have been rude of him not to do that, Doctor. That's nothing to be upset about."

"But Naomi..." his lower lip was trembling, "then my wife said to me, 'Armando and I are flying to Lisbon tonight, Leonard. I wish there were time for you to get to know him, but life is short and I know him pretty well, so I'll vouch for him. I know you'll be fine...I know in your heart you care deeply for me. It's just your medical training that's gotten in the way of our having an intimate relationship. I thought if you met him, you'd feel better about all this.' Lisbon, for God's sake...my wife doesn't even speak Portuguese."

"Perhaps Armando does, Doctor. I'm sure they'll be fine! Actually I hear that now there's practically nowhere in the world you can visit where English isn't spoken."

"But then...then she said, 'There's a meatloaf in the oven, and I made your favorite Jello mold. I can see you're upset, Leonard, so Armando and I won't stay for dinner. Perhaps a little "time out" would be good for you.' And Armando picked her up...PICKED HER UP...and carried her out the door. He came back for the suitcases in the hallway, and then they were gone."

"What is it, Doctor...was the meatloaf too dry? Remember, it's our intentions that count. I'm sure her wish was to fix a nice meal that would please you."

"No, it wasn't the meatloaf, for Chris'sake! Good God, woman...don't you have any sensitivity for my feelings? For what I'm telling you here?"

"I'm sorry, Doctor, but my hour seems to be up...now, honestly, don't you feel a little better? Just dry those tears, pick yourself up, and get that sweatsuit laundered. We'll continue right here next Tuesday."

She pulled the cord on the window shade and sunlight poured into the room.

She picked up her purse and patted the doctor on the shoulder as she headed for the door. She couldn't bear to look at his face. She worried that perhaps even the shoulder pat might have been going too far.

Chapter 12
the Flying Cows

The school year was coming to a close at Mayfield High, and it was a nostalgic time of year for Mrs. Billingsley. She had always enjoyed the activities remembered from her own high school years. Those times were now a somewhat distant memory, but as her daily life seemed to be on a happy, steadily upward path, the thought had occurred to her that perhaps there was a way she could again be of service to the young people of her community.

The Rotary Wives Club had offered the opportunity to do so, and Mrs. Billingsley had, over the last few weeks, increased her involvement with the group. The presentation of the annual Rotary Wives Club Science Award was to be made in a few days to the most promising young graduating student. The judges' committee had concluded its deliberations, and the job had fallen to her to contact the losers and let them down gently.

She had cheerfully agreed to perform the difficult duty because she felt confident that she could bring the necessary sensitivity to the task and share some of what she considered good news as she notified the runners-up.

She was making great progress, working with Dr. Birnteller on her own emotional psyche, even though his at the moment seemed to be struggling, and felt she might be able to now help other people deal with theirs. This was important, because disappointment is a strong emotion, and a seventeen-year-old genius who knows how to build his/her own hydrogen bomb, for instance, even if only in theory, is the wrong person to disappoint or offend in any way.

Thanks to donations from some of the local business-men, a laboratory had been established in the spare room at Bumble Bee Pharmaceutical courtesy of Mr. Billingsley's boss, and the runners-ups would be offered the opportunity to continue there with their own individual experiments. This prestigious honor, she felt, would ease the disappoint-ment each of them might feel at not winning first place.

The first student among the runners-up on Mrs. Billingsley's visitation list was Emiline Kreuger. All she knew of the Kreugers was that they lived on the edge of town and operated a small dairy and egg farm. What she didn't know was that Emiline was a tall, gangly girl with an austere, brooding personality and a rather sharp tongue.

Mrs. Billingsley pulled into the dirt driveway of the Kreuger farm. It was not exactly a state-of-the-art establishment. The barn was old and poorly maintained; the milking was still done by hand; the cows looked a bit scruffier than cows should, and Mr. Kreuger's chickens had free run of the place, which meant that they often got trampled beneath the hooves of the returning herd in the evening and, more importantly and problematically, chose to hang out in the barn, unload-ing their chicken shit dangerously close to the milking pails. Fortunately the milk from the Kreuger farm was sold to a nearby dog biscuit plant. There had been no recent epidem-ics in the canine community, so apparently no harm resulted from the co-mingling of these ingredients.

Mrs. Billingsley parked in the shade by the front porch and knocked at the screen door. A rather tired-looking woman with greying hair came to the door and peered suspiciously through the screen. It seemed the Kreugers didn't receive many visitors.

"Yes?" said Mrs. Kreuger, wiping her forehead with the bottom of her apron.

"Mrs. Kreuger, my name is Naomi Billingsley, and I'm here to speak with Emiline about the Science Award."

"Oh, my, yes, do come in, please! Emiline will be so pleased to see you. It must be good news, you coming in person like this!" She opened the screen door, beamed at Mrs. Billingsley, and ushered her enthusiastically into the parlor, offering her a seat on a rather worn, slightly soiled sofa with throw pillows made from chicken feed sacks. She took off her apron and sat down opposite Mrs. Billingsley.

"I'm mighty relieved to see you, Naomi...honestly, we've been awful worried about Emiline, what she'd do if she were to lose this competition. She's been real edgy and depressed, hardly speaks to her father and me. We never doubted for a minute that she'd win...she's so bright and all, but just in case, we did make plans for her to stay up with my sister and continue with her bassoon studies..."

Mrs. Billingsley interrupted her as gently as possible. "Mrs. Kreuger, I'm afraid you don't understand. Emiline's project was extremely interesting to the committee, but..."

"Oh, I know...she does seem to have a real gift. Of course, her father and me don't understand most of her little experiments, but we're real proud of her...how rude of me, Naomi—let me just call Emiline, and I'll get us a nice glass of lemonade."

She went to the bottom of the stairs and called up. "Emiline, dear..."

"I'm busy, Ma!" came the surly reply from the distance.

"But dear, Mrs. Billingsley from the Science Award Committee has come by to speak to you. She's come all the way out from Mayfield. Please come down, dear."

Rather quickly, Emiline appeared at the top of the stairs. She had lived for so long with the dream of winning the Science Award that it had become a foregone conclusion in her mind, and actually receiving the news was tantamount to accepting an Oscar. She posed at the top of the stairs a moment, removed her horn-rimmed glasses and placed them in her overalls pocket, and as gracefully as was within her ability given her severe nearsightedness, glided down the rickety stairs to the parlor.

"Mrs. Billingsley," she said, extending her hand stiffly, as if she were trying to discourage an autograph-seeker from getting too close.

"Emiline, dear, I'm so happy to meet you, and I do want to speak with you, but I'm afraid your mother has misunderstood something..."

"How perceptive of you. She misunderstands most everything. I've learned to live with it, but it must be quite a shock for you, on your first visit like this. You'll get used to it."

At that moment, Mrs. Kreuger returned with a tray of lemonade and some homemade cookies. She offered the tray to Mrs. Billingsley and Emiline managed to commandeer a few of each kind as the tray went past her.

"Emiline, dear, Mrs. Billingsley has some exciting news for you!"

Mrs. Billingsley was trying to smile through this dreadful turn of events. Best to get it over with quickly, she thought, and tried to muster up some enthusiasm, which she hoped might prove to be contagious.

"Emiline, I do have some most exciting news. The committee this year, because of the extraordinary talent that was exhibited by all the applicants of the Science Award competition, has established a special corporation. There will of course be only one first prize winner, as is customary, but..."

"Cut the crap, Mrs. Billingsley. Did you bring the check? I'd like to have it now, and you can just hand me an empty envelope at the awards assembly."

"Emiline, I'm so sorry to disappoint you, dear," Mrs. Billingsley groped around in her mind for the right words, "but, although it was terribly close, the committee felt that the award should go to Darryl Jones this year. However, let me explain the opportunity that the runners-up have been given. Here's how it will work..."

Emiline slammed her lemonade down, splashing a bit on the wooden table by the couch. She glared at Mrs. Billingsley from beneath gnarled and angry eyebrows. "Darryl Jones won? That little twerp? Everything he knows about science he's learned from watching Mr. Wizard! Does this mean he's getting the five grand?"

"I'm afraid so, Emiline." Mrs. Billingsley was frustrated. Things were not going well. If only she could reach this child. "But, dear," she continued, "Bumble Bee Pharmaceutical has donated a fully equipped laboratory on its premises where you will all be welcome to work, day or night. You will each have, you know, your own Bunsen burner...and a locked steel file cabinet where your wonderful ideas will be safe and secure. This is a wonderful opportunity, Emiline, and a young woman with your promise, well...the profits that could come to you because of this generous opportunity..."

Emiline smiled placidly. She seemed to have drifted off into some kind of trance. She spoke calmly to Mrs. Billingsley. "I've prepared for this turn of events, Mrs. Billingsley. You know, with a little nurturing, I could have gone on to great things, but with a mother who never understands anything and a father who never liked me, well...they joined forces and finally succeeded in ruining my life. I should have known it would happen. But I can accept this news, Mrs. Billingsley, don't you worry, and I merely have to move to Plan B. A well-prepared and chronically disappointed person always has an alternative plan. I have a surprise for you and my mother. Something else I've been working on. Perhaps it's something that could be developed in your little laboratory. It's kind of complicated to present and I need your help. Ma, I'm going out to the barn. When I leave the living room, will you and Mrs. Billingsley count to one hundred and then flip on the porch light?"

"Of course, dear," her mother replied, still trying to remain cheerful.

Mrs. Billingsley thought the poor girl was actually taking the news rather well, looking ahead like this so optimistically to the next project. Youth has such a remarkable ability to spring back, such an un-crushable spirit. Things would work out after all.

Emiline put her horn-rimmed glasses back on and walked out the front door toward the barn. Mrs. Kreuger looked confused, but still interested and supportive. Mrs. Billingsley had begun to count. Emiline crossed the dirt driveway and walked through the overgrown patch of brown weeds that her mother optimistically referred to as the front lawn. She disappeared through the barn door, chickens scattering as she swung it open to enter.

"Forty-seven, forty-eight..." counted Mrs. Billingsley under her breath obediently.

Mrs. Kreuger continued to look interested and confused. She looked out at the barn for a moment. She glanced toward the dining room where Emiline's bassoon case usually stood. The spot was empty. Then she remembered Emiline had taken it out to the barn earlier that morning. She had questioned her as to why, as Emiline usually practiced in the parlor on those rare occasions when she practiced at all. But Emiline had suggested that her mother buzz off, and further added that she had her own plans for the bassoon's future. As this recollection came to mind, Mrs. Kreuger began to look a bit more uncomfortable and a little less confused.

"Seventy-one, seventy-two..." Mrs. Billingsley continued.

Coming from the barn there began to be a stirring, a restless lowing. It is a little-known but true fact that cows are very extra-sensory creatures. They often behave most peculiarly when an earthquake or other natural disaster, for example, is imminent.

Mrs. Kreuger noticed the growing restlessness. Was Emiline tormenting the poor cows again? She sometimes swore the child had been inflicted upon them as a result of a hospital mix-up. It seemed like Emiline possessed not one kind or caring bone in her gangly, mean-spirited body. Goodness knows Mrs. Kreuger had tried her best to be a good mother. But somewhere, she must have failed. Then she thought again about the bassoon. Maybe...maybe Emiline was just going out to get it, to play a nice piece for Mrs. Billingsley...

"Ninety-five, ninety-six..." counted Mrs. Billingsley.

"Wait just a minute, Naomi...I think..."

But it was too late. Mrs. Billingsley stood with her hand poised on the light switch, counting down. "Ninety-eight, ninety-nine, one—" and as she turned the light switch on, she finished, "—hundred."

The wood plank flooring of the living room shook, and the glass pane windows rattled in their frames as the rumble and then the crashing sound rang out. The two women watched in horror as out across the yard the barn flew in a hundred different directions. Bits of ancient siding, bunches of hay, rusty milking buckets all danced against the backdrop of cloudless blue sky. Chickens spun through the smoky air, and Mrs. Billingsley swore she saw the bell of a bassoon flying amid the hurtling debris. The smoke rose higher and higher, and then only the occasional pitiful whimper of a distraught cow could be heard.

Mr. and Mrs. Kreuger, inconsolable despite the strained family relationships that had formerly existed, later swore that it had to have been an accident. Emiline had simply and finally attempted a feat beyond her capabilities. Mrs. Billingsley asked herself over and over if anything she could have done differently might have changed the outcome for Emiline.

After a good deal of soul-searching, she concluded that the answer was probably not. The following morning, she notified the supervisor at Bumble Bee Pharmaceutical to put the equipment for the laboratory on hold, and suggested to the Science Award Committee that perhaps next year they might include some psychological evaluation testing, along with the various other aspects of the competition.

Chapter 13

Early Tinnitus & *the* Peach Pit

Mrs. Billingsley couldn't shake the upset from her experience at the Kreugers' farm a few days earlier. She stood by the window at the kitchen sink, peeling a peach. The peach had rested on the windowsill for several days ripening, and if it remained there any longer, it would soon pass from ripe to rotten. Never one to miss a life lesson, she pondered for a moment on the significance of this and drew the conclusion that "All forward motion leads ultimately to decay." Succinct. The simplicity of her insight pleased her. Perhaps a needlepoint pillow was in order.

She continued to develop her theory. She had once read that the results of some study had proven that living things age more rapidly in warm temperatures. Not just peaches, but things with living tissues, such as humans and animals. Eskimos live longer than Polynesians, and so on, was then a logical conclusion, she assumed. Then she thought about the fact that she often eased the discomfort of her occasional neck tension by lying on a heating pad. Would her neck and shoulders, then, rot out before the rest of her? How conclusive had these studies been, how reliable? And the question logically followed, if indeed this part of her physical anatomy disintegrated before the rest of her body, would it eventually fail as an effective conduit between head and body, mind and heart?

She took her cup of coffee and her freshly peeled peach out to the veranda. This train of thought could drag her down the tracks for the rest of the morning, and it was beginning to depress her. A good subject for exploration with Dr. Birnteller, she thought. She flashed for a moment on the memory she'd tried to distance herself from; of the day she had brought her garbage along to discuss it with him. Understanding more clearly now that garbage was a metaphorical term, she knew she would not necessarily have to bring the peach pit with her to her next appointment, but it could be a good jumping-off place for the conversation.

She finished the peach and put the pit in her jacket pocket, grabbed her purse, and headed out the door. She was hoping Dr. Birnteller could help her deal with the events at the Kreuger farm. She couldn't shake the sadness and the feeling that, somehow, the incident was her fault. Perhaps if she had handled the news differently. But she had thought in circles for two days, to no avail. Now she would try to address it with a professional.

Again, Mrs. Billingsley waited in the outer office until ten minutes past the hour and began to worry a bit. But she heard something coming from inside the office, something she couldn't identify, and she thought perhaps her timing was off, so she waited patiently. She heard something that sounded like polka music, but she couldn't imagine why that would be, so she dismissed it as some form of early tinnitus. How interesting, she thought, *when one is open to the creative forces around us, even the things that can go wrong can go right.* Or something like that.

The door finally opened, and the doctor motioned her into the inner office. He seemed not quite himself, but Mrs. Billingsley understood that having shared the sad events that had occurred between his wife and Armando, he might be feeling a little embarrassed, so she tried not to even think about it, lest he pick up the energy and become distraught again.

"Good morning, Doctor. I wanted to talk with you today about the accident out at the Kreuger farm... I wonder if you might have seen the article about it in the paper?"

"Good grief, yes. Unfortunate. What did you want to discuss in relation to that?"

"Well, I'm afraid it was all my fault. You see, I went out to the farm to let their daughter Emiline know that she had only been a runner-up for the Science Award, and..."

"And she blew the barn up. Perfectly understandable. There will be good days and bad days, Mrs. Billingsley, as we've discussed. That obviously was a bad day. We must move on."

"But that's the thing, Doctor. Her parents believe it was accidental, that she didn't really mean to..."

"Nonsense. She was a bright girl. Not bright enough to win first prize, which of course is enough to make someone want to commit suicide. It happens. Unfortunate that she took all the cows and chickens with her. But sometimes, like those cows and chickens, we are just in the wrong place at the wrong time. Ours is not to judge. What else may I help you with?"

"Do you think I could have changed the course of events if I'd handled giving her the news differently, Doctor?"

"You could have lied, Mrs. Billingsley. Sometimes we have to lie to spare people's feelings. Eventually she would have learned the truth. We always learn the truth somehow. And so she would have eventually blown up the barn. The good news is that, with the course of events unfolding as it did, she had an audience. It's important when one makes such a strong point that there is an audience to feel the impact."

"I see." Mrs. Billingsley sat quietly for a moment.

"Shall we explore some other areas of distress? Have you ever felt a frustration about self-expression in your own life?

Have you ever suffered a similar disappointment? I normally wouldn't share my own personal experiences, but we've already crossed that threshold. For instance, I wanted to be a musician when I was young. My parents would have none of it. I would have given anything to have bravely run off, joined a band, auditioned for Lawrence Welk, anything, to experience the joy of making music. But unfortunately, it was not to be. My parents were bullies. No, I had to go to school, years and years of school, so I could get smart enough to sit in a room and listen to other people's dreams and frustrations. How do you feel about *that*, Mrs. Billingsley?"

Mrs. Billingsley looked at him. The tables were turning again. She didn't quite know how to respond.

"Well, I'm grateful to you for the work we've done, Doctor. And perhaps that helps me to understand what the Kreuger girl did. Perhaps she just couldn't bear the thought of giving up her dreams and didn't believe she had it in her to achieve them. So for her, perhaps blowing up the barn was exactly the right thing to do. And perhaps I needn't feel so bad about it. Perhaps I need to remember that events themselves are not problematic, but only our view of them." She paused, and then decided to take a chance. "And have you heard from your wife and Armando, Dr. Birnteller? Did they arrive safely in Lisbon?"

"Mrs. Billingsley, is there anything else I could help you with today?"

Mrs. Billingsley thought for a moment. Then she said, "Yes, Doctor, I have this peach pit in my pocket..."

Chapter 14

the New Neighbors

It was a lovely morning, and Mrs. Billingsley took her mug of coffee and the newspaper and went out to sit on the wicker swing, thinking she would enjoy for a few moments the burgeoning flora and fauna of the front yard. It had truly blossomed into the showplace of the neighborhood. It was amazing what a proper irrigation system and ten or twelve thousand dollars of landscaping could do. Even Dr. Birnteller had applauded her efforts, though the sad state of his marital relationship—or lack thereof—seemed to be making it difficult for him to discuss the happy state of her relationship with Mr. Billingsley, or much of anything else. She tried to be sensitive and focus on other things. So she had thought perhaps a conversation about "All forward motion leads ultimately to decay" might be right up his alley. But apparently, he was not in the mood. The session had ended on a somewhat down note.

Before long, a large U-Haul moving van rumbled down the street and turned into the driveway of the house next door. The house had been on the market for sale for quite some time with no results, and finally the owners had bent and advertised it for lease. Mrs. Billingsley was curious about who her new neighbors were to be. Apparently, this was moving day.

The U-Haul van pulled toward the front of the house and stopped near the front door. The driver got out, stretched his road-weary form, and then went around to the back of the van and unlocked the rear doors. A young woman climbed out from the passenger side. Mrs. Billingsley tried not to be obvious about staring at them, but she did manage to observe discreetly through the vines at the end of the veranda that the young woman had long, stringy hair and a pale, under-nourished look about her. She wore a wilted cotton frock that fell to about six inches above her ankles. Birkenstock sandals completed the somewhat time-warped quality of the picture. The driver of the truck was a slightly overweight but mus-cular-looking man, dressed in black denim, with hair that looked like it had been dyed a sort of mahogany brown. On his wrists he wore black leather cuffs decorated with silver studs. When he walked toward the front door, Mrs. Billingsley could see a patch of pale scalp peeking through the back of his head.

My, she thought. Not exactly the sort of neighbors one would choose if one were selecting from the New Neighbors catalog. But not being one to fall victim to snap judgments, she determined that as soon as the move-in process got under-way, she would take a tray of lemonade over and introduce herself.

The couple fumbled for a moment at the front door, try-ing various keys, then succeeded finally in opening the door and disappeared inside.

After a short while, a car pulled up in front of the house and parked on the street. Two burly fellows got out, went up to the front door, and knocked. The man who had driven the moving van opened the door, and they all sort of slapped each other on the back in a macho version of masculine hugs. With some pride, the man then escorted his two friends in through the front door. A short time later, all three men came back outside and began to unload the van.

Mrs. Billingsley noticed that the things they were carrying up into the house were a rather eclectic assortment of items that didn't seem to really belong together. But then neither did

their owners. After the furniture and boxes had been transported inside, the movers guided a heavy motorcycle down
the ramp from the back of the van and pushed it gently to the
garage at the rear of the house. They treated the motorcycle
with infinitely more care and affection than they had handled
any of the household items.

Mrs. Billingsley decided it was time to roll into action.
She left the veranda and went inside to make some lemonade. She freshened her makeup, spritzed herself with a bit of
her new Jungle Gardenia cologne, and carried the tray with
the frosty pitcher of lemonade and four glasses out to the
veranda, down the steps, and across the driveway. She bal-
anced the tray on one hip and knocked at the door of her
new neighbors' house. In a moment the door opened, and
the mousy young woman stood smiling at her through the
screen door.

"Hello there...I'm your neighbor, next door. My name's
Naomi Billingsley...my husband and I live over there in the
house with all the vines. I thought you and your movers
might enjoy a bit of cold lemonade. You've been working
so hard...I'll just leave the tray here on the porch. Welcome
to the neighborhood, and don't hesitate to knock if there's
anything you need while you're getting settled," she said as
warmly as she could manage. Then she continued, "Don't be
afraid of the birds...they're harmless, though they do have
rather mean squawks."

"Well, thank you so much, Mrs. Billingsley. That's awful
nice. I'll get my husband...won't you come in?"

"Oh, no, dear, I know how hectic things are in the middle
of a move. When you get a bit more settled, I'll come over for
a cup of..."

She stopped mid-sentence. The tall, mahogany-haired
man with the black wrist cuffs appeared suddenly behind the
young woman, glowering at her. The young woman acqui-
esced to give him center position inside the screen door
and said a little tentatively, "This is my husband, Ivan, Mrs.

Billingsley. Ivan, honey, this is our new neighbor, Naomi Billingsley. She just brought over this nice pitcher of lemonade. Wasn't that sweet?"

The young woman's southern drawl, which Mrs. Billingsley hadn't noticed at first, was becoming decidedly more pronounced.

Without changing his glower, the man's eyes accosted Mrs. Billingsley's body through the screen door. She could feel it, even though she was unaccustomed to receiving this kind of attention. She tried not to notice, but the blatancy with which he explored her breasts and then the rest of her was difficult to ignore. It was almost as though he was intentionally trying to make her uncomfortable.

"Nice to meet ya. Why don't ya come on in, Naomi? Real neighborly of you. Don't s'pose we could borrow a cup of vodka, could we? I never drink this stuff straight." He continued to leer as he opened the door and smiled a little, amused at his own joke, then raised the pitcher of lemonade as if in a toast.

"Oh, no, thank you. I really can't stay. But welcome to the neighborhood." She thrust the tray into his hands and turned to leave, wishing she had told the young woman that the birds were rabid and there were crocodiles hiding under the vines.

"Thank you, Naomi. We'll bring the tray back over this evening," the young woman called after her.

"No need, no need. We've got plenty of trays," Mrs. Billingsley replied hastily. And she hurried down the porch steps and back across the driveway to the safety of the tropics. *Mercy,* she thought. Mr. Billingsley won't find much to kibitz about over the back fence with Ivan. Pity. The Sugarmans had been such pleasant neighbors.

Chapter 15

Leila Mae *& the* Brownies

Mrs. Billingsley, because it was part of her daily life and, as such, was under scrutiny along with everything else, had eventually discussed her new neighbors with Dr. Birnteller. Aside from Ivan's gruff persona, there was very little unusual about them, really. It was just strange to have a motorcyclist living next door. But she would adapt, the doctor assured her.

She had really tried to put the initial meeting with her new neighbors out of her mind. They had rather gotten off on the wrong foot, and there had been little contact since, save an occasional wave across the driveway as she pulled her car into the street. She rarely saw the wife, but "Ivan the Terrible," as she and Mr. Billingsley had taken to calling him, spent a lot of time tinkering with his motorcycle in the driveway between their houses.

One day as she was placing apple slices on the veranda railing for the toucan, she saw Ivan leave on his motorcycle, helmet and black jacket indicating it was for more than a quick jaunt to the 7-Eleven. She decided to take his absence as an opportunity to walk over for the once-promised cup of coffee and get a better look at the young woman. This had seemed such a strange coupling, and her instincts told her that Ivan's young wife might welcome a little civilized companionship from the outside world.

She took off her apron and went inside to get her latest copy of *Good Housekeeping,* thinking she would offer it as a gesture of goodwill. There was a nice article about hot weather recipes that looked fairly simple, and it seemed appropriate to share. A moment later she was knocking on the door.

Soon it opened a smidgen, and the young woman peered through the screen.

"Oh, Mrs. Billingsley, how are y'all? I swear I been thinking 'bout running your pitcher back to you...I don't know where the time goes! Me 'n' Ivan was just sayin' the other night how we wanted to have you an' Mr. Billingsley over for drinks and maybe a little game of cards. I'm not quite settled, you know, but I just knew you'd understand. About the mess, I mean. Won't you come in?"

"If you're sure I'm not disturbing you, dear. You know, when we met on moving day, I never did get your name... please forgive me...I don't know what to call you."

"My name's Leila Mae Trowbridge, Naomi. I'm pleased to meet y'all again!" She opened the screen door for Mrs. Billingsley and ushered her inside.

The living room was still cluttered with unopened boxes. An overstuffed sofa stood against one wall, and on the opposite wall were several units of sound equipment, stacks of CDs and videos, and a very large screen television set with complicated looking gadgets and wires weaving all around the floor. Near the couch was a Naugahyde recliner chair with motorized vibrator controls on the arm, and next to it a dusty coffee table strewn with bottle caps, a large ashtray with cigarette butts spilling over the edges, and a directory of cable T.V. channels. The room was rather dark, as the shades were half-drawn. Mrs. Billingsley's eyes took a moment to adjust to the dimness.

"I brought you this magazine, Leila Mae...it has some real nice recipes I thought you might want to try."

"Why, that's just so neighborly...thank you! Naomi, would you like a cup of coffee? I got a pot goin' in the kitchen. We can sit at the table out there and get acquainted."

"That would be nice, Leila Mae. Thank you."

The two women walked to the rear of the house, through a dining area with a card table and folding chairs featured in the center of the space, above which hung a crystal chandelier left over from the Sugarman era. Along the wall were four large metal file cabinets and the card table was strewn with papers and another burgeoning ashtray. Mrs. Billingsley thought perhaps the Trowbridges ran some sort of business out of their house. She could ask about that, and it would give them something to talk about over coffee.

Leila Mae filled a flowered mug and handed it to Mrs. Billingsley, then topped off her own white mug and sat down at the table.

"So, Naomi...do you mind if I call you Naomi? It's so nice of you to come by. We don't know many people yet, and I get sort'a lonesome when Ivan gets busy with his projects. You know how men get so absorbed in their work. Leaves a lady to her own devices. Where we lived before, I had a good job workin' at the hospital, but Ivan says he'd rather I didn't work here. Says he likes to have me home when he gets through at the end of the day. He's kind of old-fashioned, but he's really very sweet."

"Old-fashioned men can be very special, Leila Mae."

"I was hopin' you'd come by when he was home so you could get t'know him better...he was kinda tired after all that movin' when we met you the first day, and I'm afraid he wasn't too friendly."

"On the contrary, Leila Mae...he was extremely friendly." Mrs. Billingsley cleared her throat and continued, hoping she hadn't been too obvious about her discomfort the day they'd met. "I just don't like to intrude on folks when the man of the house is home. You know, a man's home is his castle, they say."

"Oh, you're so right, Naomi. Ivan says that all the time. I wish he'd look for some office space to rent so we can move all that stuff out of the dining room and enjoy our little castle!"

"Does Mr. Trowbridge operate his own business?"

"Yes, he does, Naomi." Leila Mae's brow twisted into a quizzical expression. "I don't exactly know what it is he does, but he works real hard at it. He fills those little padded envelopes and stamps 'em, and sends 'em off, and every day he spends hours and hours at his table there. He was doin' such interesting things back in Paris. The neighbors didn't seem to like us much, but you know sometimes people's buttons kinda get pushed. He keeps to himself and thinks a lot, and I know sometime Ivan is gonna come up with something truly salvational for mankind."

"Oh, then you lived abroad?" asked Mrs. Billingsley, grasping at the glimmer of hope that these people might be diamonds in the rough.

"Abroad?" replied Leila Mae, confusion showing on her sweet young face.

"In Paris?" Mrs. Billingsley smiled.

"Oh, dear me, no," laughed Leila Mae. "Paris, Texas, Naomi. Me and Ivan lived in Paris, Texas, for about one and a half years. 'Fore that we lived in Waco, and 'fore that we lived in Tennessee. Mama worried lots when I told her me 'n' Ivan was goin' to Texas, but I believe a wife should follow her husband and stand by his side even when there's trouble. I learned that from my mama."

"Trouble?"

"Yes, Naomi. She stayed right by my pa, even though..." Leila Mae seemed to have stumbled across a painful memory. She grew quiet for a moment. Then she continued. "Well, then after me an' Ivan got together, it just seemed like everywhere we went, people didn't understand Ivan. You know, we suffered with police harassment all the time! One day two officers showed up at the door and talked to Ivan for a long time, and that night he says to me, 'Leila Mae, we're gonna pack up and move out'a here. It's gettin' so a man can't live his life without pissin' off some old busybody...'"

"Oh dear, Leila Mae..."

"Oh, excuse me, Mrs. Billingsley, but that's just what he said. He usually don't talk like that, but he was real upset. We packed everything up...we didn't have a whole lot to pack then...just newly married and all. And we rented us a truck that night at U-Haul and we just left. We didn't say goodbye to no one. We just drove straight on through to Paris."

"It must have been difficult for you, moving so frequently. I hope you have a chance to stay in Mayfield long enough to get acquainted. It's a really pleasant place to live, and the community has so many activities and organizations that you and Mr. Trowbridge might find interesting." She was hard-pressed to think what those might be at the moment, but she did want to be encouraging.

"Oh, Ivan's not much of a joiner, Naomi. He gets nervous when folks get too friendly. I just try to go along with it, but sometimes I wish we had some nice friends, you know, like you and Mr. Billingsley. Ivan's okay if folks don't talk to him too much about his business, but he's a real private kind of person, if you know what I mean."

Then Leila Mae brightened a bit. "Um, Naomi, I have some delicious brownies I just baked last night. Why don't I get us some to have with our coffee?" She winked at Mrs. Billingsley as she got up from the kitchen table, and continued talking as she reached up into the cupboard for the tin of brownies. "These are kinda special brownies, Naomi. You don't have anything pressing to do this afternoon, do you?" She giggled and brought a plate of moist, dark chocolate brownies to the table. The sweet aroma wafted up into Mrs. Billingsley's nostrils. She had started her diet again this morning for the fifth time this month, but perhaps just one, to be gracious. She wouldn't want to hurt Leila Mae's feelings.

"Thank you, dear. They look delicious." And she helped herself.

The two women sat nibbling together over their coffee, chatting. As they visited, Mrs. Billingsley felt herself growing more at ease, and felt quite enthusiastic about her new friend. Leila Mae asked about Mr. Billingsley and about Mayfield, and soon the conversation flowed gaily, interspersed with laughter and a fresh supply of brownies.

Finally, after most of the small talk seemed to have been exhausted, Leila Mae suddenly leaned across the kitchen table and took hold of Mrs. Billingsley's arm.

"Have you ever thought, Naomi, about just packing up and going off to find some adventure of your own? You know, just going to the bank and taking out all your money and leaving Mr. Billingsley with the cat to feed and all the bills and just buyin' yourself a pretty new wardrobe and going off to maybe San Francisco or even New York City? I think about it lots, Naomi. Sometimes I lie awake at night thinkin' about it. But I never get brave enough to do it."

Mrs. Billingsley was a little taken aback. She thought about the question. She looked out of Leila Mae's kitchen window across the drive to her own house, with its new climbing blossomed vines, and her little vegetable garden in the backyard, where one of the parrots sat on a pile of dirt pecking at her tomato plants. She thought about it some more. She really couldn't see it...running off from it all...for herself. But she suddenly pictured Leila Mae in a stylish new outfit, suitcase in hand, walking out the door, shutting it on Ivan, and going off to Chicago. She decided Chicago would be better for Leila Mae than San Francisco or New York City. She pictured her sitting in a smoky jazz club in Chicago, sipping a sloe gin fizz next to a handsome young man with patches on his jacket elbows and a notepad in front of him. The young man was a music critic for the Chicago Tribune, and he was crazy about Leila Mae. They would leave the smoky jazz club and walk together to their apartment overlooking Lake Michigan. Leila Mae would take some classes in the eve- ning...perhaps a wine-tasting class and a discussion group of American Literature of the Twenties. She would cut her stringy blonde hair, have it restyled, and she would make espresso after dinner in a smartly decorated apartment for herself and the handsome music critic. Mrs. Billingsley, in the passing of mere moments, created an entire new life for Leila Mae. She smiled as she basked in the satisfaction of her accomplishment.

Her reverie was interrupted by the sound of giggling. Leila Mae was poking Mrs. Billingsley with her forefinger and giggling uproariously.

"Naomi, I didn't say you could leave *now*...I was just ask- ing if you ever *thought* about it. You just up and left me sittin' here all alone with my brownie crumbs. I think you do think about it, don't you!" She patted Mrs. Billingsley on the shoul- der in a congratulatory manner.

Mrs. Billingsley blushed. "Oh my goodness, dear. I did wander off for a minute, but I was thinking about you going off to a new life, with bright young friends and an exciting place to live..." Mrs. Billingsley wondered if she should speak so freely. But, inspired in the moment, she continued. She would seize this opportunity to fertilize the seed of an escape plan, which was obviously already planted in Leila Mae's thoughts, and help her get out of this wretched dilemma in which she lived.

"Leila Mae, do you have a checkbook?"

"Those brownies really did go to your head, Naomi. Ivan wouldn't no more give me a checkbook than he'd loan his Harley to some stranger."

"Well, where does he keep his money? How do you pay your bills?"

"Ivan likes to deal in cash. He says cash is the only thing

you can count on these days. All those little envelopes you saw in the dining room? They come in with dollar bills in them. Ivan, he takes those dollar bills and puts them in a wooden box that he keeps by his side of the bed. Even when he goes off on his bike and has his meetings and comes home with his 'big bucks,' like he calls them, he deals in cash."

She leaned close to Mrs. Billingsley. "Naomi," she whispered, "you want to see? I know where he keeps it but I don't ever touch it, 'cause he knows exactly how much is in there. If I was braver, I'd wait 'til he was gone, and I'd grab me a handful and I'd take off. But I wouldn't never really do that 'cause Ivan would get so mad. I'd be scared to think what he'd do if he ever really got mad at me."

Mrs. Billingsley looked at Leila Mae. There was such a frightened look in her young eyes, like an animal on the run. She felt an urgency; a concern for this sad young woman whose life seemed to be at the mercy of the strange man in black wrist cuffs. His whole existence reeked of suspicious motivations.

"Leila Mae, you don't have to be afraid of him. You have rights, you know. Half of everything he has belongs to you. You don't have to live your life cowering in fear. You're such a pretty thing, and so sweet, and you're a person too, you know. If he doesn't treat you well and you ever need to, well, you know, make a change...make a decision to leave, you just remember you have a friend now right next door, and she'll help you any way she can."

Leila Mae looked at Mrs. Billingsley. Tears began to well up in her eyes and she reached into her apron pocket for a handkerchief.

"You don't know how much that means to me, Naomi. I never would really go, but just knowin' you're there means a whole lot to me. I used to think if I ever got real tired of Ivan I'd call my mama and she'd send me a bus ticket back to Tennessee. But Mama's gone now. She got pretty sick last winter, and before I could get Ivan to let me go home and see, her Aunt Millie called and said she just passed away that night over at the hospital. Awful sudden. And we couldn't go home just then, and now I sometimes feel like I'm all alone in the world. But since I got me a friend now, Naomi, that makes Mayfield a real special place." She reached over and gave Mrs. Billingsley a hug.

"My goodness, look at the time, Leila Mae. Where has the afternoon gone to? I must be getting back home to fix Mr. Billingsley's dinner. You'll come over to visit me next time. Thank you for the delicious brownies...you'll have to give me your recipe."

"They have a special ingredient in them, Naomi. Ivan gets it for me. They're from a recipe he says his mother used to make. I'll ask him to get you some."

When Mrs. Billingsley got home, she sat on the veranda for a few minutes in the wicker love seat swing, thinking about Leila Mae and Ivan. She wondered just how hard it would be to find the music critic with the patches on his elbows.

Chapter 16

the Toucan &
the Faceless Man

Several more weeks passed uneventfully. The friendship between Mrs. Billingsley and Leila Mae deepened, with the two being frequent visitors in one another's kitchens. Leila Mae did seem terrified still at the prospect of Ivan finding out about their bonding, and was careful to plan her visits for periods of time when she knew Ivan would not be likely to arrive home unexpectedly and find them together. The card game between the two couples never took place, for one rather flimsy reason or another. Mrs. Billingsley had to admit she was not terribly disappointed about that.

But she had been having strange dreams. And they repeated. And they were all about Ivan. However, not in the normal way people dream about someone. These had to do with untimely demises, Ivan being the untimely demise-ee. In one dream, the large pet toucan swooped down on Ivan from the Billingsleys' front porch as he was trying to break in through their front door in the dead of night. The bird attacked him viciously, its large, sharp, hooked beak gouging holes in Ivan's face and sending him off screaming into the night. In another, Ivan was again trying to break in the front door, and the vines that twined around the railing of the porch sprang to life like snakes, wrapping themselves around him, pulling his hands behind his back and twisting around him, then creeping up toward his neck and choking him. Just as he began to scream in that dream, Mrs. Billingsley woke up, her heart pounding. This wasn't right, she thought. But at least if she couldn't confront him in the light of day herself, the toucan and the vines were stepping up to take care of things. She decided the new landscaping and exotic bird acquisition had been a good investment.

Mrs. Billingsley also had experienced something rather strange. When she went into town for tropical bird food at the pet store, or stopped at the library, or just ran into the market, she kept seeing a tall young man kind of in the distance ahead of her, walking with the crowd. He would be wearing a tweed jacket with patches on the elbows, and always carried a notepad in one hand. But then at some point he would turn around to look back toward her, and he had no face. She couldn't figure out how he found his way around Mayfield with no face, no eyes to see. And then he would be gone. And then a day or so later, she would see him again. She thought of course that it was the young music critic she had conjured up, who would rescue Leila Mae and run off with her to Chicago to their apartment and the wine tastings, and finally, when she saw him one more time, she waved at him. And he waved back. She couldn't figure out how he knew to wave back, since he had no face and no eyes and had no idea that someone had waved at him. But she decided it was not her responsibility to figure it out. She wondered if she should tell Leila Mae about him. Maybe the next time they had coffee and brownies.

The visits next door did continue, when it had been sufficiently determined that Ivan was elsewhere. One afternoon, Mrs. Billingsley was next door helping Leila Mae cut a dress pattern out of a bright pink and lavender floral cotton print. They were on their hands and knees in the middle of the living room floor when the sound of the Harley rumbled in the distance and grew louder, obviously coming down the street toward the house.

"Oh, Lord, Mrs. Billingsley, that's Ivan. What'll I do? He's been askin' me every day what I do and where I go, and I haven't been telling him nothing 'bout our visits because he was startin' to get so riled up. He just don't seem to like people, Naomi..."

"It's all right, dear, don't be concerned," Mrs. Billingsley said, trying to calm her. "I will just explain that I just popped in, uninvited and..."

"No, you don't understand. He don't like to have anyone knowin' my business. I told him you were different, not a busybody or anything like that. But he'll know I've been lyin' to him. I told him I was going to the dentist this afternoon and then over to the mall. He's goin' to be so mad! Naomi, would you mind hurrying home out the back way? Then I can just tell him I decided to do some sewin'..."

The motorcycle was now in the driveway, the motor revving, and then silence.

Leila Mae's heart pounded. "Oh, Naomi, it's too late. Maybe I could say you just came over to borrow a cup of sugar... yes, that's what I'll tell him." Just then the front door opened and Ivan walked into the living room, his black crash helmet under one arm, black leather gloves in hand, wiping the sweat from his forehead.

"Leila, baby, get me somethin' cold...goddam clown who was supposed to meet me never showed, and..." He saw the two women on the carpet huddled over the pink and lavender cotton flowers. "What's this?" he asked, glowering at Leila Mae.

"Oh, honey, it was so hot I thought I'd just stay home and do some sewin' and then Mrs. Billingsley just knocked a minute ago 'cause she needed some sugar for the cookies she wanted to make..." Leila Mae stammered. She spoke a little too fast, and a little too cheerfully.

"That's a funny place to keep the sugar, Leila Mae." He spoke harshly to her, as if he were reprimanding a small child.

"Oh no, honey. She was just showin' me how this pattern would fit better if I turned it around, see, like this..."

"I thought we talked about this. Better give me the scissors, baby. Thanks, Mrs. Billingsley, for dropping in. Leila Mae'll get you your sugar." He took the large cutting shears from Leila Mae, who surrendered them meekly and went dejectedly into the kitchen, returning with a cup of granulated sugar.

"Thank you, dear," said Mrs. Billingsley, taking her cue from Leila Mae. "I'll bring you back some cookies when they're done," she said as she turned to leave before she found herself in the middle of an unpleasant domestic scene.

"Bye, Naomi. Don't worry about the cookies. Me 'n' Ivan been trying to cut back on the sweets a little. I'll talk to you soon."

Chapter 17

Let's Write *a* Musical About Death

Several more weeks passed. Mrs. Billingsley felt she should deal with the anxiety she was feeling about these new neighbors, and particularly Leila Mae's plight with this difficult fellow. She tried to get a sort of chronological sequence of events in her mind so she could explain the situation to Dr. Birnteller at her appointment that morning. And when he opened the door and welcomed her in, she was surprised to see he had an accordion strapped on his chest.

"Ah, Mrs. Billingsley, and how are we this morning?" the doctor exclaimed. He sat down in his Eames chair and began playing a little jaunty tune. Mrs. Billingsley was a bit confused and tempted to ask about it, but since there were other things to talk about this morning, she tried to overlook the accordion. Perhaps he was trying out a new approach to exploring the subconscious.

"We are fine, Doctor, but I'm afraid the young woman next door to me is not so fine. I'm worried about her, and it's causing me to have disturbing dreams."

"Well, perhaps we should talk about them. Do proceed. And I will play just a gentle underscore while we talk. Nothing too lively, but I think we'll both find it soothing. Please continue, about the dreams."

"Very well." She remembered the doctor's comments a week or so back, about his longing for music, and then remembered the sounds coming from his office that she attributed to early tinnitus symptoms. *So that is what this is all about,* she thought. She tried to refocus.

"Well, the dreams are about the toucan attacks, and then there is the faceless man..."

The doctor began to pick up the tempo of the tune he was playing on the accordion. "Toucan attacks, you say? And a faceless man?" And he intensified the pumping of the accordion bellows.

"Yes, Doctor," she continued, raising her voice a bit in order to be heard above the accordion. "I keep seeing him around town, dressed in his jacket with the patches on his sleeves, and carrying his notepad. At first I thought he had come to rescue Leila Mae, the young woman next door, from her tawdry life. But he has no face. That seems problematic, don't you think? And he just keeps disappearing into the crowd."

"Mrs. Billingsley, I think we've had the good fortune to have stumbled upon fascinating material—I think you and I could make something out of this. I think there's a song here somewhere...possibly a whole musical..."

"Doctor, I don't mean to be disrespectful, but that seems to be rather off track in terms of what we're supposed to be doing here this morning, don't you think?"

"Not at all, Mrs. Billingsley. I was most appreciative of your kind help the other day, when you found me somewhat disturbed over my wife and Armando. But then it dawned on me; this is a creative effort, a two-way street. There's a lot of great material going on here in this room, Mrs. Billingsley. I finally got my accordion out—you know I haven't played for years—and having so much time on my hands at home now in the evenings, it does lift my spirits. And I remembered the course I took in college on music of the theater. It's all based on life, you know, someone's life...and I thought what could be more interesting than *your* life, Mrs. Billingsley? And then I realized we have a wealth of musical material here, as co-writers, because we have, in a way, recreated your life together, wouldn't you say?"

"Very well, Doctor." She wasn't sure exactly what that implied, but she did want to get on with the conversation. The tempo slowed down on the accordion, and the doctor leaned in as Mrs. Billingsley tried to stay focused.

"When I finally decided that it was not my place to try to understand the purpose of his presence—the faceless man—I just relaxed and waved at him the next time I saw him. And he waved back, though I'm sure he had no idea who he was waving at. Which made me consider the possibility that a faceless man could see out, even if we could not see in, even if he had no face, no eyes..."

Dr. Birnteller set his accordion down and reached for the pad on his desk. He quickly scribbled down the words "The Toucan and the Faceless Man, by Leonardo Birnteller and Naomi Billingsley." Then he turned back to her.

"Mrs. Billingsley, you have just touched upon the very basis of all psychological work. Whether we understand the purpose of *anything* is immaterial. As we have said many times, 'acceptance of all things is what gets the clutter out of our lives and allows us to move on.' I am trying to look upon the end of my own failed marriage as a form of de-cluttering." He picked up the accordion, went back to playing, and continued to speak.

"We'll continue our work next week, and if I haven't come up with the right melody yet, I will call to reschedule. Next week we'll explore your thought that a faceless man could see out, even without eyes, which when you think about it, is really quite deep. And might work as the climax of Act II."

Even though it was only twenty-five minutes past the hour, Mrs. Billingsley accepted his dismissal without objection. She was having a hard time holding onto the trust she had come to place in Dr. Birnteller this morning, and besides, the accordion was beginning to grate on her nerves, which was not the purpose of psychotherapy at these prices.

Chapter 18

Leila Mae Leaves

Several weeks had passed, and Leila Mae never came over to see Mrs. Billingsley after the incident with Ivan and the cup of sugar. Mrs. Billingsley had gone next door only once, on a sunny weekend when Ivan had disappeared on the bike for what she assumed might be a "road trip" day. Leila Mae had seemed distracted that day, their visit brief and their conversation superficial. She talked nervously about nothing, asking questions of Mrs. Billingsley about her life before she married Mr. Billingsley. She seemed to want to escape into someone else's life. She smoked continuously and her eyes darted frequently to the front yard like a scanner, watching for Ivan's unwelcome approach. She assured Mrs. Billingsley several times that nothing was wrong, but she seemed anxious for the visit to end. Mrs. Billingsley finally excused herself, fearful her presence was causing the young woman distress. Leila Mae walked her to the front door, and as she was leaving, she asked Mrs. Billingsley if she might borrow some cutting shears to finish cutting out the flowered dress, which had been abandoned since Mrs. Billingsley's last visit. Ivan had put hers somewhere and she hadn't been able to find them.

Mrs. Billingsley cheerfully offered to go across the drive and get them, but instead Leila Mae went with her and waited on the veranda until she came out with the scissors.

A week or so after this exchange with Leila Mae, Mrs. Billingsley realized there had been a distinct lack of activity next door, especially over the last twenty-four hours. She thought perhaps Ivan and Leila Mae had taken a little trip someplace, and finally, after much consideration, decided that she would risk being once more an unwelcome visitor and would pop over to be sure everything was all right.

She walked across the driveway, up to the Trowbridges' front door, and reached up to knock on the frame of the screen door.

The inside door was ajar, just an inch or two. Mrs. Billingsley knocked lightly, and when there was no response, knocked again. It was not like Leila Mae to go out and leave the door open. She was much too aware of Ivan's disapproval to do anything that careless. Perhaps she was working in the kitchen and didn't hear the knock. Mrs. Billingsley opened the screen door, pushed the front door open another few inches, and called inside.

"Leila Mae? Yoo-hoo, dear...hello?"

There was no response. She stepped inside.

The living room shades were drawn, the house silent and dimly lit. Mrs. Billingsley stepped back outside and walked toward the rear of the house to see if Leila Mae might be in the yard. Something felt unsettled, out of place.

She knocked on the back door. "Leila Mae, it's Naomi, dear...are you there?"

Still no reply. She turned the door handle and opened the door effortlessly. The kitchen was quiet. An ashtray stood on the kitchen table, surrounded by an overflow of ashes. Dirty dishes were strewn about the counter, along with bits of trash, fast food containers, and several empty beer cans. It was unlike Leila Mae to let things get quite so out of hand.

Mrs. Billingsley walked through the tiny dining room, where the card table was still piled high with papers and clutter. The living room was heavy with the stench of stale cigarette smoke.

Magazines were scattered on the floor, and a dirty coffee cup sat on the coffee table next to another overflowing ashtray. The place obviously hadn't been tidied in days.

On the floor by the front door there was a small canvas suitcase, and tossed over the back of the chair was Leila Mae's navy-blue acrylic knit poncho and the tooled leather shoulder bag she carried whenever she went into town. Relieved, Mrs. Billingsley called out once more. At least she had happened in before Leila Mae made her getaway. She could bid her an affectionate goodbye, wish her luck, and extract a promise from Leila Mae that she would stay in touch. She had not realized until that moment how attached she had grown to the young woman.

"Leila Mae, I'm so glad I caught you before you..." Her voice trailed off as she turned through the hall doorway into the front bedroom and stumbled over the small wooden box lying on the floor, open and empty, just inside the doorway.

Then she saw Leila Mae. The girl was sprawled across the unmade bed, her long hair tangled and covering her face. The cutting shears lay on the floor, fallen from the lifeless hand that dangled over the edge of the bed, and a red stain spread over the bedclothes.

"I sort'a been expecting you, Mrs. Billingsley."

Ivan spoke low and haltingly in an emotionless tone. He was sitting in an armchair by the side of the bed, staring mindlessly at the young woman's body.

Mrs. Billingsley stood in the doorway, her heart pounding. Frozen in shock, she was unable to move, run out of the room, or go to Leila Mae's aid. But something told her it was too late for that.

"I couldn't let her leave, Mrs. Billingsley. I been tryin' to take care of Leila Mae. I know you thought I wasn't very good to her, but you don't know all the story. I should have told you, maybe. I know you cared about Leila Mae. But I couldn't take a chance. I was glad she had you for a friend,

Mrs. Billingsley. But you shouldn't have let her have those shears. She don't never mean nothin' bad, but she can't help herself. See, I knew I could keep her from hurtin' anyone else, and I would'a kept us on the move if I'd had to. But if she went off alone, she would'a hurt somebody for sure, and then they would have taken her away again. She would have been so frightened, Mrs. Billingsley. She knew I'd take care of her. I had to stop her from leavin'. And she just went kind of crazy when I stopped her. She ran in here and locked herself in, all upset and cryin'. And I thought she'd eventually settle down. She finally did, and I thought she'd just fallen asleep and I'd talk to her in the morning. But in the morning it was still so quiet, and she wouldn't answer me. I had to break the door in. It don't matter whether you tell anyone now. It's all over."

Ivan slumped in the chair. He looked half the size of the tall, threatening man Mrs. Billingsley had encountered that first day at the screen door. His eyes were swollen and red.

"What do you mean, Ivan...she would have hurt somebody? Leila Mae wouldn't hurt a fly..."

"Oh yes, Mrs. Billingsley, she would have tried to again, anyway. We had to leave Tennessee on account of what happened. Leila Mae just couldn't take it anymore. I think what happened with her pa drove her right out of her mind. They never did nothin' to him. Her mama was afraid to tell people what he'd done. We lived next door to them, back in Tennessee, my family and me. Leila Mae was just my little sister's age, and the sweetest thing I ever knew. But there was just something so sad about her. Even back then I knew I was takin' a chance stayin' with her. She got troubled in her mind and tried something again in Paris. Little girl, lived next door. Leila Mae was babysitting. I should have known better'n to let her be there alone, but everything had been so peaceful and Leila Mae was doin' so good after her stay at the hospital. I came home just in time. Everything was okay, but the little girl was screamin' so, and we just had to run. I feel like we been runnin', Mrs. Billingsley, 'til there maybe wouldn't be no more places to run to. I couldn't let her take off by herself. I couldn't do that."

Mrs. Billingsley turned away from Ivan and Leila Mae. Her thoughts were all running together, and she had a hard time at first, trying to understanding what Ivan was telling her. She didn't know what to say to him. Finally, she touched his arm gently, shook her head as the tears came, and said softly, "I'm so, so sorry, Ivan..."

Then she just left them there, the two of them alone together as they had been for so long, and walked out of the bedroom, out of the little house, and back home across the driveway.

Mrs. Billingsley placed the receiver of her kitchen phone back in its cradle. She went outside through the front door and sat in her wicker swing on the veranda. After a few minutes she heard the sound of sirens approaching, and minutes later an ambulance pulled into the driveway next door.

She pushed the ground with her toes and set the swing in motion. She thought about appearances. She thought about secrets. She thought about the music critic with the patches on his sleeve. This time he had a face, and she could see it clearly. And it looked an awful lot like Ivan's.

Chapter 19

Billy Randall *& the* Reunion

The leaves were starting to turn to gold and auburn on the trees that lined the streets of Mayfield. Fall was in the air, the Sugarmans' house next door was empty again, a "For Rent" sign once more on the front lawn, but there was a deeper emptiness that Mrs. Billingsley was feeling inside. Maybe this was life, she thought, once the nonsense was cleared away, once you stopped trying to understand it and just watched it go by, knowing and accepting that there was not much you could do to affect it. You could fill your own life with tropical plants and preening, brightly colored birds, and you could involve yourself with the community and even make friends with the people next door, but you couldn't keep their lives from crumbling, if indeed that is what they were fated to do. You couldn't keep barns from blowing up, and you couldn't deny the fact that your psychiatrist may be just slightly less sane than you, his patient.

She had canceled her last two appointments, finding it difficult to face the accordion accompaniment she was at risk of hearing from Dr. Birnteller, as the story of Leila Mae and Ivan inevitably would have to unfold. So she decided to give herself a brief "time out." After all, she had made a great deal of progress, and there were other things to consider in life.

For instance, earlier in the week the announcement had come that the graduating class of Mayfield High School, Summer '52, was holding its thirty-year reunion, and volunteers were requested. Mrs. Billingsley responded, thinking it would take her mind and emotions in another direction, and offered to serve on the welcoming committee. Her shift at the door was rather late in the evening, from eight to nine p.m. She had selected the shift because the chances of anyone actually arriving at that hour were slim, and she was *not*.

She had mixed feelings about the event. It offered the possibility of renewed friendships and familiar faces, a sharing of happy memories in a festive atmosphere. But her insecurity began to resurface, and she felt the commitment to serve, but later in the evening, would enable her to be on the defensive throughout the earlier evening, ever nimble-footed and alert, to quickly dart behind a potted palm should an old rival or arch-nemesis suddenly appear, looking absolutely divine.

She did get back on track with Dr. Birnteller, in a sort of "maintenance" every-other-week schedule, claiming budgetary limitations. He agreed to set the accordion aside, as other tenants in the building had been complaining about the disturbance anyway, but he seemed disappointed to hear that the faceless man had disappeared and there were no more violent dreams about the toucan. His mind wandered when she told him what had happened with Leila Mae, and he made a few new notes and congratulated her on how well she handled the situation. She asked him which situation, and he explained that specificity was unimportant; that his comment was just in reference to the handling of reality in general.

Mrs. Billingsley did discuss the approaching reunion with the doctor, and he pointed out that sometimes we make progress by going backward in order to go forward, and so the reunion would be a positive therapeutic experience.

What she did not share with the doctor was that in her secret heart, Mrs. Billingsley prayed for two things regarding the reunion. She prayed to be able to lose ten or fifteen pounds by the November 12th date, and she fervently prayed that the reservations committee had been able to locate Billy Randall.

Billy Randall was the one that got away. He had been the star quarterback (in those semesters when he'd managed to make his grades and was allowed to play), the president of the Student Body, the president of the Junior Red Cross, the first in their crowd to lose his virginity (although unhappily, not with her), the first to join the Marines, the first to make her a marriage proposal...and the first to marry someone else.

She blamed herself for that, though. His proposal had come over the phone as she bustled about at the soda fountain where she worked at Klemer's Drug Store. He had called her from Marine boot camp at Camp Pendleton, having come to the certainty that life with Naomi was what he longed for. And she was thrilled. That is, until she thought about the fact that she was only seventeen at the time, her parents would be heartbroken if she did not go to college as they had planned for her to do, and further, Billy was Catholic, and she could never adapt to that particular faith. Beneath all of that, she of course later realized, was that she was terrified of committing to adulthood that early in her life. When she eventually got brave enough to address all these issues with him, sadly, he turned abruptly and resolutely in another direction.

She'd saved all his letters from Marine boot camp in a little pine box, and she had danced at his wedding with a warm- spirited, kind young man who was sensitive enough to realize and respect the pain she was experiencing at the time and had agreed to accompany her to the event.

Actually, many years after marrying Mr. Billingsley, she'd opened that precious pine box and reread the letters. It was somewhat comforting after all those years to find that the limitations Billy demonstrated in terms of vocabulary and spelling were profound. Odd, that she hadn't noticed this at the time, although she did remember being in the habit of carefully choosing her words, lest he misunderstand her the first time around.

She was forced to admit to herself that life with Billy Randall, once they moved from the back seat of his '48 Chevy into more permanent quarters, might have proven disappointing. Surely though, Billy would eventually have made his mark in the world in some extraordinary way. His gift of connecting to others should mean that by now he must be no less than a congressman, or quite possibly even something a bit more profitable. His charm would carry him over the rocky spots where limited intelligence and lack of formal education alone might have failed him. That smile would have taken him through a lot of portals. She knew that his first marriage had fallen apart after a rather short time, but then she had lost track of him.

She imagined him walking up behind her at the reunion on this remarkable evening of revisited passions, imagined him speaking her name softly and sweeping her out onto the dance floor to the nostalgic strains of "Mr. Wonderful" sung by Peggy Lee, as she turned to look up into his blue eyes.

She realized, of course, that this was purely her childhood fantasy, and that no one could have been more perfect for her in reality all these years than Mr. Billingsley. She would never want to hurt his feelings, and knew her life was on track as it was supposed to be...nonetheless, in preparation for the possibility of this happy encounter, she decided to undertake a rigorous training program. She cut down to eight hundred calories a day, she bought a new grey jogging suit and matching headband, and she committed to jogging two brisk miles a day, rain or shine. She also meditated, focusing all of her powers of concentration on shrinking her molecules, just in case the reduced calorie thing didn't work. Miraculously, all of the aforementioned efforts combined, in less than eight weeks, to create a new sylph-like form and an equally lightened spirit within her.

As the weeks passed, Mrs. Billingsley's confidence under-
went a renewal. Finally, as the day of the reunion approached,
she found herself wishing she'd signed up for an earlier shift
at the door. She had shopped for a new cocktail dress and
found something quite lovely in gold lame with one shoulder
exposed, Grecian style, and a form-fitting bodice that set off
the new waistline of which she was so justly proud.

In the afternoon the day of the event, Mr. Billingsley washed
and waxed the car, and Mrs. Billingsley spent the better part
of an hour rummaging through boxes in the garage to find
the pair of Angora dice she had made for Billy Randall. He'd
returned them to her upon their break-up, as honor dictated
in those days, along with the St. Christopher medal she'd
given him when he left for boot camp. She had saved them
along with the pine box filled with his letters. She found the
dice and hung them from the mirror in the Buick, hoping Mr.
Billingsley wouldn't ask for too many details.

Mr. Billingsley presented her with a gardenia wrist cor-
sage, remembering that it was her favorite in the days when
they used to go dancing out at the lake. They made quite a
handsome couple still, she in her golden gown and he in a
rather snug-fitting but nicely tailored tuxedo. She was just
a tiny bit concerned that an encounter with Billy Randall
might be upsetting to Mr. Billingsley, but this evening was in
some way a step out of the present, a pause in the evolution
of time. She had the feeling that, should the moment come,
there would be no one else existing in it but herself and Billy,
so there would be no irreparable harm done.

Mayfield Hills Country Club sparkled with the excitement
of the big night. The class of '52 had arranged for valet parking
for the evening, an amenity not customarily provided by the
club. Great attention was given to detail, and walking into the
main area of the club was like stepping back in time to the gym-
nasium of Mayfield High on the night of the senior prom. The
velvet tones of Nat King Cole singing "Darling, Je Vous Aime

Beaucoup" floated through the air from a distance to greet them as they picked up their name tags at the check-in table.

Inside, the music suddenly was a bit livelier, and several middle-aged, slightly overweight couples danced under the reflective, circling centerpiece that hung above the dance floor. Mrs. Billingsley scanned the room, looking for familiar faces, but of course, there weren't too many, as faces tend not to stay familiar with the passing of decades.

After a few minutes, faces did begin to come more into focus, the years peeled away, and Mrs. Billingsley found a table of three couples that welcomed them enthusiastically; Betty Brower and her husband Bob Tice, now an orthodontist with offices in both Mayfield and the neighboring town of Norton Spring, Sandy Hall with Frankie Perez, who everyone was sure would end up in the Mexican mafia but apparently had gone into the construction business instead, and Susie and Harry MacGregor, who everyone knew would get married and stay married forever.

Betty, Sandy, and Susie had all been part of the Cebonettes, along with Mrs. Billingsley. That was the social club that the popular girls belonged to in the eleventh and twelfth grades. She was deeply aware that the only reason she was voted in (you had to be voted into the Cebonettes) was because of Billy Randall. Billy was also the only reason she was chosen as one of the cheerleaders. It helped if your boyfriend was the star quarterback. Well, that was okay. That was just how things were done in those days. Betty Friedan and Gloria Steinem had changed all that, thank goodness. Women could stand a bit more on their own achievements now. But in the fifties and sixties, you had to play the game according to the rules.

As the evening began, the group chatted away, brought back drinks from the bar, and caught up on the intervening years. Mrs. Billingsley declined the offer of a cocktail, thinking to keep her mind clear should she run into Billy. She tried to casually scan the hall as the evening wound on, but dinner was over, she had served her post at the door, it was now nearly nine o'clock, and there was no sign of Billy. Maybe they just hadn't been able to locate him. She thought perhaps she would just excuse herself, slip out to the ladies' room and on her way, stop by the welcome table to double-check if Billy's name was indeed even on the registry list.

As she rounded the corner of the hallway toward the ladies' room, she nearly had a head-on collision with Harvey Cohen. She hadn't seen him in years but recognized him immediately. "Harvey, oh my goodness! How wonderful to see you!" They hugged, and the wheels started to whirr inside her brain. Because Harvey had been such a close friend of Billy's, she was sure he would know the latest.

"Harvey, I was just going to see if Billy Randall had checked in yet...have you seen him?" she asked, in as nonchalant a manner as she could muster.

"Oh doll, sorry, I guess you ain't heard. Billy passed away... oh, y' know, very sad...maybe fifteen or twenty years ago."

Mrs. Billingsley tried not to show the jolt the news had given her. She shook her head and said, "No, Harvey! Are you sure? What happened?" Harvey was the world's biggest gossip, even back in the day, so she was pretty sure he would know the details. At the same time, she knew that being a gossip, he would want to spread any tiny fact he had heard as confidently as if it had just been in the headlines of the *Daily News*. So maybe he was wrong.

"Naomi, I know this is gonna be tough for you to hear, 'cause you and Billy was quite an item at one time, but uh... word is, Billy died of Aids. I'd kinda lost touch with him. I don't know if he had a change of lifestyle, y' know, or if maybe it was drugs, and the needle thing, but—that's the story I heard, from a pretty solid source."

Mrs. Billingsley just stared at him. She couldn't quite make the connection in her head. This wasn't the Billy Randall she knew. No, this had to be wrong. And if the cause of death was wrong, then maybe the whole *idea* of death was wrong.

And Harvey was such a gossip, he probably just grabbed hold of this story because it was a wild one, one that would get him points for knowing some really "hot stuff" about an old school mate. Harvey never could be trusted, that was just a feeling she'd always had about him. No, this had to be all wrong.

"You okay, Naomi?" Harvey was looking at her, kind of concerned.

"Oh yes, yes, I'm fine...just a little surprised at the news, Harvey. Well, we never know, do we, where the road will take us after we leave those early years. Well, you take care now, you hear?" And she hurried down the hall and into the ladies' room.

Fortunately it was empty. She looked at herself in the mirror. The tears were starting to come, and she dabbed at the corner of her eyes with a piece of paper towel. She thought about the phone call from Billy, just a few years after graduation, when his marriage had broken up and he'd reached out to her. By that time, of course, she'd met Mr. Billingsley and things were pretty serious. But it had quickened her heartbeat, hearing his voice. He'd moved to the East Coast, was working as a lifeguard at some fancy hotel near Miami, and he'd said to her that if things ever didn't go right for her, that he'd always be there, just to give him a call. That didn't sound like someone with a drug problem. That sounded like a solid, loving citizen. It didn't sound like someone with a lifestyle change either. This story of Harvey's couldn't be true. Mrs. Billingsley walked back toward the main ballroom, but then on the wall where some posters and announcements were hanging, she noticed a poster that said "IN MEMORIUM." It was a listing of the classmates who had passed away since the last reunion twenty years earlier. She hadn't noticed it when she and Mr. Billingsley had checked in, nor when she stood by the table greeting folks as they arrived. She walked closer to it and scanned the list of names. "William Nathanson...Patricia Pearlman...Richard Peters...Billy Randall..." She stopped reading.

The entrance door in the lobby of the country club was

open, and she stepped outside into the cool night to catch her breath. She stood for a few moments under the starry night sky, her mind whirling back to another time, to another sky, another night.

Billy Randall had come back from boot camp and surprised her on the doorstep of her family's home. He was so handsome, so proud and ready to face the world, a brave Marine come home to claim his beloved. She could see his face just as clearly as if he were standing there before her now in the moonlight. Then she realized there *was* someone standing in front of her. It must be one of the young valet parking attendants, she thought.

"Yes ma'am, do you have your parking ticket?"

But it was Billy's voice. She looked up. It was Billy's face.

Billy winked at her and said, "I told you I'd always be here if you needed me, Naomi. You're beautiful as ever. You made the right decision, though. I just came to say goodbye...it's all okay now."

And he was gone. She blinked and looked up and down the drive and around the doorway area, but she knew she would not find him.

It was just as Dr. Birnteller had said. Sometimes we make progress by going back in order to go forward. Mrs. Billingsley brushed away a tear, then turned and went back inside. She wandered the halls for a while, stopped in the ladies' room again to be sure her makeup wasn't smeared, and then headed back into the ballroom and looked for the table where Mr. Billingsley was sitting with their friends.

"There you are, my dear! We were beginning to worry that someone had run off with you!"

Mrs. Billingsley kissed him on the cheek, gave him a hug, looked into *his* big blue eyes, and said, "I hope it's not too late—I think I'll have that cocktail now."

Chapter 20

Physician, Heal Thyself

It had been five weeks since the Mayfield High School reunion. Mrs. Billingsley was enjoying the renewal of friendships with her three high school friends, and she, Sandy, Susie, and Betty were meeting again for lunch. It was a festive time of year—the main street was strung with Christmas lights, the windows beautifully decorated to inspire holiday shoppers, and the ladies had chosen a special French restaurant, a bit extravagant perhaps, but this was to be their special holiday lunch.

It wasn't one of the bi-monthly Fridays on which Mrs. Billingsley would normally go for her appointment with Dr. Birnteller, but she had a little gift she wanted to drop off for him before the Christmas weekend, so she planned to stop on the way to lunch. Just a token, really; some of her special home-baked holiday pastries. It was to be a rather bittersweet visit too, because Mrs. Billingsley was realizing that for the most part, she had accomplished her goals as far as the work with the good doctor was concerned. It's difficult to know when that work is done, but lately it seemed the issues with which life presented her were things she felt more able to deal with on her own. And too, there was so much wisdom from those early days with him that had just become almost a part of her DNA. The words sprung up when they were most needed—things like "sometimes we have to fall back to move forward," "therapy works when you least expect it to," and "events themselves are not problematic but only one's view of them." Life itself was a kind of therapy, so you just had to live it and watch what happened along the way.

But she didn't want to let go of all the magic. There had to be, once in a while, a little escape from reality. It seemed lately that she and the doctor were meeting on middle ground—he finding his way back to his own magic, and she dangerously close to losing the ability to find hers.

Just for the sake of old times, she decided to wear her tweed suit with the velvet collar and the little hat with the veil. Though she didn't need the veil for any practical reasons, she thought the bird might enjoy a holiday outing.

She finished dressing, carefully applying her makeup as she knew the other ladies would be on top of it. And of course, the aura of the French restaurant required it. Then she signed the little gift card that went with the tin of baked holiday treats and headed for town.

She found a parking place very near the entrance to Dr. Birnteller's building. How fortunate, she thought, what with the holiday crowds out and about. She could just run in and say hello or, if he was busy, press the light button and leave the package by the door.

She took the elevator up to the seventh floor. Christmas music flowed through the speakers into the little space. This was such a delightful time of year, she thought. She exited the elevator on the seventh floor and walked down the hall toward Dr. Birnteller's office. But there was a note on the door of his office:

"To the Patients of Dr. Leonardo Birnteller: My apologies. I will be out of the office for an undetermined length of time on a prolonged sabbatical. The pressures of daily practice have caused emotional stress. If you need referrals, please contact Dr. Damon Intrabartolo. 1-800-777-9292

PS – Should you have need for music for private holiday parties, weddings, funerals, or other functions, Dr. Birnteller is available and will provide accordion music, with appropriate costuming."

Mrs. Billingsley was stunned. She had no idea things had gone this far. But somehow, it felt right. We all need to pursue our dreams, she thought, even if we get to it a little late in the journey.

She had a bit of time to spare before she was to meet the ladies, so she unwrapped the package of pastries and took a brownie from the artfully arranged tin. She walked back toward the elevator and sat down on the carpeted floor in the hall, leaning against the wall, remembering the first day she had come to Dr. Birnteller's office. She had arrived early that day and had sat there by the elevator waiting for him because the building was new and there were not yet any names on the doors of the offices. She nibbled on the brownie and smiled, remembering it was Leila Mae's recipe she had used. What a shame that Dr. Birnteller wouldn't have a chance to enjoy them. But that first day, when he stepped off the elevator and she looked up at him, it was a bit like watching the Pope step onto the balcony of the Vatican. She had heard so much about him, and she knew nothing about the *probing* of the subconscious, just that she had a very *active* one, and that it might be ripe for probing. And indeed it had been. But one thing she had learned was that no one is infallible, not even the Pope. And definitely not Dr. Birnteller.

She could send the pastries by mail to the office address. Surely, they would be forwarded. And perhaps, she thought, on the way home from lunch with the ladies, she might just at least *look* for the "To Central America" exit again. It had been such a long time.

ABOUT ATMOSPHERE PRESS

Founded in 2015, Atmosphere Press was built on the principles of Honesty, Transparency, Professionalism, Kindness, and Making Your Book Awesome. As an ethical and author-friendly hybrid press, we stay true to that founding mission today.

If you're a reader, enter our giveaway for a free book here:

SCAN TO ENTER
BOOK GIVEAWAY

If you're a writer, submit your manuscript for consideration here:

SCAN TO SUBMIT
MANUSCRIPT

And always feel free to visit Atmosphere Press and our authors online at atmospherepress.com. See you there soon!

ABOUT THE AUTHOR

In addition to her singing performances and work as a vocal contractor/choral director, **SALLY STEVENS** has had her short stories, poems and essays published in *The Offbeat, Mocking-heart Review, Raven's Perch, Hermeneutic Chaos Literary Journal, The Voices Project, Los Angeles Press, Between the Lines Anthology: Fairy Tales & Folklore Re-imagined, Funny in Five Hundred, The Missouri Review* and *No Extra Words* podcast.

Milton Keynes UK
Ingram Content Group UK Ltd.
UKHW012146040124
435404UK00004BA/139